The Grind

The Grind

BLACK WOMEN AND SURVIVAL IN THE INNER CITY

ALEXIS S. MCCURN

RUTGERS UNIVERSITY PRESS
New Brunswick, Camden, and Newark,
New Jersey, and London

Library of Congress Cataloging-in-Publication Data

Names: McCurn, Alexis S., author.
Title: The grind : black women and survival in the inner city /
Alexis S. McCurn.
Description: New Brunswick, New Jersey : Rutgers University Press,
[2018] | Includes bibliographical references and index.
Identifiers: LCCN 2017059093 (print) | LCCN 2017061774 (ebook) |
ISBN 9780813585079 (epub) | ISBN 9780813585086 (web pdf) |
ISBN 9780813585062 (cloth : alk. paper) | ISBN 9780813585055
(pbk. : alk. paper)
Subjects: LCSH: African American women—Social conditions. |
Poor African Americans—Social conditions. | Urban poor—United
States—Social conditions. | Urban women—United States—Social
conditions. | Inner cities—United States. | Sociology, Urban—
United States.
Classification: LCC E185.86 (ebook) | LCC E185.86 .M3938 2018
(print) | DDC 05.48/896073—dc23
LC record available at https://lccn.loc.gov/2017059093

A British Cataloging-in-Publication record for this book is available
from the British Library.

♾ The paper used in this publication meets the requirements of the
American National Standard for Information Sciences—Permanence of
Paper for Printed Library Materials, ANSI Z39.48-1992.

www.rutgersuniversitypress.org

Manufactured in the United States of America

For my mother, Sharon C. McCurn

CONTENTS

The Grind

Introduction

I FIRST MEET Mecca in May 2008.[1] A black woman in her early twenties who stands about five feet five inches tall, she has a creamy medium-brown complexion and wears her natural hair beneath wigs of different styles and lengths. On the day we meet, her wavy, mahogany-toned hair lies long against her shoulders. She is struggling to carry a baby stroller up the stairs to her second-floor apartment. As I watch her struggle, I notice two middle-age Latinas and one black teenage boy walk by; they act as if she's not even there. I put my backpack down beside the first step and holler up to her, "Ma', you need some help?"

"Yeah!" she hollers back. I see her balance the stroller against her leg. I head up the stairs to where she is waiting, pick up her baby bag, put it over my shoulder, and grab the front of the stroller as she holds onto the back of it. Her baby son laughs and smiles at no one in particular.

"'Preciate it," she says as we make it to her front door and she unlocks its black metal security gate. "I didn't think I was going to make it, as hot as it is today."

"Yeah," I reply. "It's supposed to be in the nineties through the weekend."

"Then folks gonna get real wild, I bet," she says, and I nod in agreement.

"I'm Alexis. I live over there," I say as I point to the second-floor apartment I share with my mom.

1

"Yeah, I've seen you around. I'm Mecca," she says, "and this is Jaylen." She rubs the top of the baby's head as he sits in his stroller. "You always carrying some books or something. You go to school?"

"Yeah."

"Oh. Well, I'll see you around," she says. "Thanks for the help."

"No problem," I say as I walk away.

Over a nine-month period I observe multiple encounters unfold between Mecca, a mother of two small children (Jaylen is about nine months old, and her daughter Amira three years old, when we first meet), and the representatives of the institutions with whom she must have repeated contact to ensure the health and survival of herself and her family. Mecca and I see each other in passing, and as I conduct observations in the East Oakland community in which we live. We talk informally amid small groups of other residents, usually outside on the corner or in a driveway trying to escape the heat. We meet with increasing frequency as we become more familiar to one another over time. I observe her interactions with grocery store attendants and employees at the Check-N-Pay, a business that offers—without conducting a credit check—payday loans, cash advances, and check cashing services at sometimes exorbitant rates for persons without traditional bank accounts. Sometimes she appears defeated, as she does when she is denied a purchase in the grocery store, and other times she appears victorious. She may have been denied or harassed by a store clerk, but nonetheless she walks away appearing unfazed and not visibly angry.

I am drawn to Mecca because she is a member of the segment of the population I have come to the Bay Area to study: a poor black woman and mother of young children who lives in a distressed urban neighborhood. Her concern that because of the heat it might "get real wild" is a casual reference to the violence that characterizes the neighborhood. Her experiences, including her pain, are shared by many women living under similar conditions in poor inner-city neighborhoods throughout the United States.

Mecca and I share both similarities and differences. At the time we meet, we are both young black women living in East Oakland, a racially segregated and economically distressed urban community. Yet unlike Mecca, I have gained social capital through higher education that has changed my class status and will give me the opportunity to one day leave this community.

Over time, I come to see Mecca as representative of an often silenced and in many cases ignored segment of the American population. She is a working-poor American black woman between late adolescence and early adulthood who is managing to survive in a tough urban community. Here, survival is defined as the process of obtaining income, food, shelter, clothing, transportation, and health care.

During the first nine months of my field research I observed Mecca as she went about these tasks. I took note as to how checkers at the local supermarket talked to her as she conducted transactions with her Electronic Benefit Transfer (EBT) card, a form of public assistance that can be used to pay for food. I witnessed store clerks deny her purchases with her card. On one occasion I stood some distance behind Mecca in a checkout line at the local grocery store and watched the following encounter unfold. As I wrote in my field notes,

> I observed a late thirties white female store clerk tell Mecca, in a voice loud enough for other customers to hear, that fish and fresh vegetables were not authorized purchases when using an EBT card. When Mecca protested and told the woman that was not true, the store clerk glared at her and said in a loud, demeaning tone that this was policy and to take it up with the government. Mecca replied, "This

must be a policy at this store only, because I have never had this problem anywhere else." An older black man with salt-and-pepper hair, standing behind Mecca in line, came to her defense. He told the store clerk, "Ma'am, you know as well as I that this girl is making approved purchases with her card; why are you hassling her?" The clerk responded, "Sir, this does not concern you." Mecca, now visibly angry, asked to speak with the store manager as her young son began to cry in his stroller. The clerk said, "The manager isn't here right now, so either follow policy or go to another store." Mecca left the store with her crying baby and no groceries.

On other occasions I witnessed store employees overcharging Mecca for purchases, dropping her groceries, and demanding that she either quiet her crying baby or leave the store. I observed Mecca as she experienced a dilemma often shared by poor black women in public spaces: feeling simultaneously invisible and hypervisible. Upon entrance to the store, she was openly watched and often followed from aisle to aisle, usually by the same employees who harassed her daily at the checkout, but sometimes also by security. Others often treated her as if she was invisible when she reached the checkout counter and ignored her. When she greeted the clerk with a hello she was greeted with a look but no response. I never observed a cashier greeting Mecca first, even though I saw the same cashier greet patrons ahead of and behind her in line. Unlike other customers, Mecca was never offered help out of the store with her purchases.

Similar encounters at check-cashing stores are routine for young women like Mecca; I watched as an employee at the Check-N-Pay shoved money at her through a small opening in the ceiling-high glass barrier between them a common occurrence, as John P. Caskey (1994) and Ebonya Washington (2006) note. This same clerk often screams directions through this glass wall at customers on how to fill out forms. On one occasion, another employee at the Check-N-Pay told a black woman customer who appeared to be around Mecca's age (also with two small children) that her state-issued identification card was an unacceptable form of the ID required for her to cash her paycheck. I stepped in and offered to help the woman by speaking to the clerk on her behalf. The store employee screamed at both of us, "You girls leave the store if you don't want to follow the rules!" At the Check-N-Pay, the only formal rule made visible for customers is posted on a square plastic sign near the front of the store: "We have the right to refuse service to anyone." Informal rules and penalties, as well as who might be a rulebreaker, are determined from day to day by store personnel. For example, on one occasion I observed a woman speaking into her cell phone loud enough for me to hear from the rear of the store escorted out by security for "making too much noise." Conversely, another time I watched a man angrily address and violently threaten to "choke out" a woman who accompanied him inside the store; the man was allowed to complete his transaction and at no time was asked to leave the premises. These types of occurrences could have different outcomes depending on the discretion of employees on a particular day or at a particular time.

My observation and involvement in encounters like these helped me to uncover one of the key ethnographic findings in this book: the routine microinteractional assaults experienced by women like Mecca and the strategies they use to negotiate such encounters. Microinteractional assaults impart a range of biased attitudes and beliefs held about marginalized groups. These assaults work to attack the group identity of the targeted individual based on their gender, race, sexuality, or class status through avoidant behavior, name calling, or other discriminatory actions. Microinteractional assaults extend what Derald Wing

Sue describes as "microaggressions" as the "brief, everyday exchanges that send denigrating messages to certain individuals because of their group membership (people of color, women, or LGBTs)" (2010, 24). My analysis of microinteractional assaults complements previous scholarship by focusing on a form of social injury that occurs at the intersection of race, gender, and class and reflects the complicated experience of having more than one marginalized status while living in a distressed inner-city neighborhood. This analysis is unlike prior literature in its examination of the experiences of poor and working-class black women.

In all, I collected seventy-five cases of microinteractional assaults through fieldwork and in-depth interviews with black women in the neighborhood. Of these, forty-one cases were collected from reported accounts shared during formal and informal interviews. I directly observed the remaining thirty-four encounters that were recorded in my field notes.

My research in this setting reveals that women in poor urban neighborhoods regularly encounter harsh daily realities.[2] Under these conditions they must develop their own strategies to negotiate routine conflicts and survive. How do women like Mecca and others do this work every day? In what ways do they accomplish the routine tasks necessary for basic survival under these conditions? And, what are the consequences of their doing so?

BLACK WOMEN AND INNER-CITY LIFE

Earlier scholars have examined the lives of U.S.-born black women as individual subjects within the U.S. social order. They have been both investigated and understood through multiple externally attributed labels, or what Patricia Hill Collins (2000) describes as "controlling images" such as the mammy, the welfare mother, and the whore. Sociologists and criminologists often frame black women and girls as "social problems" or "gang girls," but have given less attention to problems they encounter in their daily lives (Jones 2010). Scholars have neglected to look at the ways in which black women manage everyday encounters and interactions individually and collectively. A systematic examination of such encounters reveals the ways in which these women negotiate survival at the level of interactions. This is consequential because these interactions and encounters are often unavoidable, routine activities that are part of the process of managing daily life.

Few scholars pay special attention to the specific strategies that black women use to negotiate encounters while in urban public space. How do intersections of race, class, and gender influence the strategies used? What are the consequences of negotiating encounters in this way? In an effort to respond to these questions it is important to examine the ways in which race, class, gender, violence, and the body are experienced, understood, and managed through everyday encounters in urban spaces. In the process of negotiating survival, these elements become central to how encounters and interactions play out in one's daily life (Fenstermaker and West 2002).

It is also important to document the individual accounts and collective experiences of black women and girls who live in distressed urban neighborhoods. It is significant to explore the day-to-day experiences of black women and their position within the larger canvas of the U.S. social order, which is central in both their personal as well as their public encounters (Ladner 1971; Leadbeater and Way 1996). Narrative accounts reveal the daily work that these women do to survive in this setting. Their collective experiences show the consequences of this work based on how others evaluate who they are as poor black women within routine public interactions. Previous scholarship has neglected to provide a multilayered examination of raced and gendered encounters within contemporary public space and advance an intersectional analysis of feminism and identity construction for black women on public display.

In this book I examine the experiences of black women in public space. I focus on their experiences in a local grocery store, a neighborhood check-cashing establishment, on the city bus, and in their neighborhood more broadly. I rely upon firsthand accounts from women and nearly two years of field research in East Oakland, California. I situate my analysis in the sociological literature on urban ethnography, black feminism, and interactional studies. I also draw on American studies literature that focuses on race and working-class populations—specifically the black urban poor. This study uncovers the varied experiences that black women have in public space and considers how these experiences inform and shape the strategies they use to survive there.

THE CREATION OF THE
GHETTO IN OAKLAND

In my field research, it was not uncommon for women to use the term *grinding* to describe the informal and formal work they did to make money; as I explain in chapter 1, the term reflects the intensity and drudgery of work in their daily lives. Why is daily life such a grind for poor black women? The answer to this question has something to do with the structural forces that have shaped distressed urban communities since the 1970s. According to Douglas S. Massey and Nancy A. Denton (1993), the black ghetto is the characteristic institutional form of racial segregation. Key structural factors such as joblessness, crime, and racial segregation are responsible for the perpetuation of black poverty in the United States. Just a few miles away from the East Oakland neighborhood where I conducted field research, neighborhoods are not infested with crime and overtaken by joblessness. The segregation that created this community in its current form also produced the racial and class isolation present there.

These systemic and institutionalized factors restrict the life chances of black women who live in this space. The shift from a primarily industrial economy to a service economy has further intensified social and racial isolation as well as residential segregation in poor communities throughout Oakland.

This "ghetto," like others nationwide, was created by predominantly white institutions and is maintained and condoned by these same institutions (Massey and Denton 1993). Urban communities have undergone considerable changes over the last several decades. The move from a primarily production-based economy to a service economy has significantly changed the race and class composition of inner-city residential communities (Anderson 1999; Jones 2008; Massey and Denton 1993; Wilson 1980, 1987, 1996). With this drastic economic shift has come "white flight" and then "black flight," both of which have seriously impacted residential neighborhoods and retail sectors. Over the course of the late twentieth century, once thriving inner-city communities became distressed and segregated neighborhoods concentrated with poor people of color.

The social ills of urban life are primarily rooted in racial inequality. As William Julius Wilson notes, "The rates of crime, drug-addiction, out-of-wedlock births, female headed families, and welfare dependency have risen dramatically in the last several years, and they reflect a noticeably uneven distribution by race" (1987, 20). Additionally, the cumulative results of racial discrimination increase the near impossibility for many blacks to take advantage of available resources. Wilson argues that central contributing factors to the steadily increasing ills of the ghetto underclass, particularly in the latter quarter of the twentieth century, include shifts in the American economy that have resulted in enormous rates of black joblessness, a historic flow of migrants, a change in the urban minority age structure, population changes in the central city, and class transformations in the inner city (Wilson 1987; see also Sharkey and Elwert 2011).

Since the 1970s, inner-city poverty has increased steadily. Between 1969 and 1982, the number of poor people in U.S. urban centers increased by 62 percent, from 13.1 million to 21.2 million. During this time the proportion of people living in poverty increased by 43 percent (Wilson 1987, 172). Wilson proposes that race-specific policy changes are not the answer to such largely structural problems. Rather, policy changes and implementation directed to solve the broader problems of societal and economic organizations would prove to be more effective. Wilson goes on to explain the key factors that led to the social transformation of the inner city: concentration effects and the erosion of what is known as a "social buffer." The term *concentration effects* "refers to the constraints and opportunities associated with living in a neighborhood in which the population is overwhelmingly disadvantaged" (Wilson 1987, 144); the term *social buffer* "refers to the presence of a sufficient number of working and middle-class professional families to absorb the shock or cushion the effect of uneven economic growth and periodic recessions on inner city neighborhoods" (Wilson 1987, 144). The bottom line is that once these middle-class families left the neighborhood, basic social institutions of the community—such as churches, stores, and so on—became harder to sustain, especially amid the increase of long-term joblessness. Over time, this negatively affected the foundation of the inner-city social organization, leading to both a lost sense of community and a decrease in positive neighborhood identification (Wilson 1987, 145).

Urban ethnographer Elijah Anderson (1990) asserts that this exodus significantly reduced a prominent source of moral and social leadership in black neighborhoods. He notes that the reason that many black families depart from the inner city is in an effort to ensure employment opportunities, class status, and even survival. The departure of the black middle class from urban centers was accompanied by a greater presence of community distress; joblessness, crime, drugs, and family disorganization become compelling forces. These pressures also exist in neighborhoods in which lower rungs of the black middle class remain, as described by Mary Pattillo (2008). Moral structures fade as a culture of alienation and crime becomes central (Anderson 1990). Consequently, opportunities to work and operate within the mainstream economy and social world dwindle.

The recent Great Recession has likely intensified the unstable conditions experienced by many poor families living in urban centers. In 2010 California's poverty rate was 15.7 percent, with nearly six million individuals living below the federal poverty level. Of African Americans in California, 22.1 percent were living below the poverty level. In Alameda County, which encompasses the city of Oakland, 13.3 percent of the county population was living below the poverty level in 2010 (Bohn 2011). This does not account for the numerous individuals and families hovering just above the poverty level within Alameda County. The onset of the Great Recession surely intensified the distress already experienced by many East Oakland residents.

Making East Oakland a Ghetto

Oakland, California, is an exemplary case of an urban community that has undergone dramatic social and economic transitions over time that have shaped the lived experiences and survival strategies of many of its residents. Oakland became more than just a rest stop for travelers when the Central Pacific Railroad selected it as the last stop for its transcontinental route in 1869. Later, when the company added sleeping cars to its trains for long distance travel, the Pullman Company began to hire black porters. By the late 1800s this last stop on the train line had become home for numerous Pullman sleeping car porters and their families. As the railroad grew, the need for more workers followed. Blacks were eventually hired as cooks, baggage handlers, laborers in the freight depots, and waiters. By the early 1900s, Oakland had a vibrant middle-class community that attracted more and more black professionals and government employees, and the success of this city and its residents grew. By the 1920s many southern blacks began to migrate there in search of jobs. Many of these families were poor and occupied any free space, including abandoned buildings, for shelter upon arrival (Kaplan 1997; Self 2003).

With the Great Depression, the economic promise of Oakland came to an abrupt halt. This time of struggle took jobs away from countless black Oakland residents; many had little choice other than to seek public assistance for the first time and at the alarming rate of four times that of whites. As some Americans were coming out of the Depression during the 1940s, the percentage of the city's black population that remained largely unemployed was over six times that of whites. During the mid-1940s the war industry offered some relief; the Oakland shipyard, Mare Island Naval Base, and the construction industry brought thousands of blacks to Oakland and the East Bay for work. As new workers arrived, the necessity for adequate housing became obvious. Due to housing segregation throughout the 1950s, many newly arrived blacks did not have the freedom to move as they pleased throughout Oakland, but were instead limited to the available housing in East Oakland. Here, there were few established community organizations and institutions like health clinics, dance clubs, churches, political clubs, and the like. All of these were paramount to support a growing community, and many of these institutions had been established in West Oakland.

By the late 1960s and into the early 1970s, the city's demise quickened as a result of the demolition of the recognized black community in West Oakland via urban renewal projects. Such projects, adopted nationwide and supported by the federal government and urban planning experts, were meant, in theory, to revitalize old neighborhoods. Yet, in practice, urban renewal often meant redevelopment, which resulted in stripping neighborhoods of low-income housing and small businesses for the benefit of industry and middle-class homes (Self 2003, 139–140). Consequently, the presence of a structured and thriving social and economic base in black Oakland quickly faded. By the late 1980s things had gotten progressively worse; the local Social Services Department reported that nearly 90 percent of single-parent families headed by women in Oakland were living at or below the poverty line and receiving government assistance (Kaplan 1997, 63).

The Failure of Redevelopment in Oakland

A new era was marked for middle-class blacks in Oakland when Lionel J. Wilson was elected mayor in 1977. Under Wilson's leadership, people of color were named to central positions in local city government. Between 1969 and 1993 the number of black city employees grew from 15 to 40 percent. By 1980, the majority of members on the city planning, port, and civil service commissions were black, Latina/o, or Asian American. By 1983, all five city council seats designated and elected by district were held by African Americans. With the rapid changes in local government, members of the conservative white middle class began to flee to surrounding suburbs.

Between 1970 and 1990 Oakland's white population declined by nearly one hundred thousand. Suburban flight did not stop the strong influence of neighboring conservatism. In 1978, state voters passed Proposition 13, which limited city government from increasing property taxes. This caused city resources to be cut by nearly $14 million; this brought substantial layoffs, service reductions, and facility closures. In turn, Mayor Wilson rallied behind the downtown City Center renewal project in an effort to shift resources to black communities through the city's redevelopment agency. The retail sector of this project was short-lived. By the 1980s major retail stores had left the city for suburban shopping malls, and large department stores such as Macy's declined offers to open stores in Oakland's downtown district. Other developers including the Bechtel Corporation also withdrew plans to build there. With the city steadily searching for new investors and developers, one large retailer admitted that it was the city's racial makeup that was not ideal (Rhomberg 2004, 183–185).

In 1990, after serving three terms in office, Elihu Harris succeeded Wilson as mayor. Harris, a long-term state legislator, continued Wilson's effort to develop downtown Oakland, including the nearly $200 million twin-tower federal building and a nearly $100 million high-rise state administrative building. Yet private investors remained uninterested, and much of the commercial retail space in downtown Oakland remained vacant. In addition to the downtown district, the Port of Oakland was also a target area for development, including the creation of new retail, office, and restaurant space. After the city spent nearly $100 million developing a portion of the city's waterfront property known as Jack London Square, much of the newly built retail space went unoccupied for a long period of time. While vacant, this cost the city hundreds of thousands of dollars each month (Rhomberg 2004, 185).

Although development was slow during this time, there was a black majority serving in local politics. Blacks held positions on the city council and the school board, and as city manager, city clerk, city attorney, head of city planning, and director of economic development. Yet the black poor and working-class segments of Oakland's population continued to suffer. Between 1981 and 1988 the city lost twelve thousand jobs in the manufacturing, communications, utility, and transportation industries. With the dramatic decline in service jobs the unemployment rate soared among the working class. The city's overall unemployment rate stood at 9.5 percent. For blacks, the unemployment rate was 14.5 percent, and in some city neighborhoods it was much closer to 20 percent. In 1989 nearly 23 percent of black families lived below the poverty level, the same as in 1979. The 1992 census reported that East Oakland was labeled as medically underserved by the U.S. Department of Health and Human Services because of high infant mortality, poverty, and lack of primary care physicians in the area (Rhomberg 2004, 186).

Harsh living conditions resulted in impoverished black communities becoming particularly vulnerable to the growing presence of drugs, crime, and violence. During the 1980s notorious drug dealers like Felix Mitchell and Milton "Mickey" Moore headed gangs and drug businesses that rose quickly on the streets of Oakland; Mitchell earned tens of thousands of dollars daily in his far-reaching heroin and cocaine sales. This dangerous business and lifestyle drew countless teens and children as runners and small-scale peddlers. By the early 1980s Oakland was experiencing over one hundred murders each year. With the rise of crack cocaine, drug sales, and violence, Oakland began to see that homicide rate nearly double by 1992 (Rhomberg 2004, chap.8). Although much of the violence, drugs, and crime was centered in poor black residential neighborhoods throughout Oakland, this growing urban distress influenced the image of the entire city, including downtown, as a "dangerous black city" (Rhomberg 2004, 187).

In 1998, after Mayor Harris declined to run for a third term, Edmund G. "Jerry" Brown, the former and now current California governor, was elected mayor of Oakland. With just two remaining black representatives on the city council and on the school board, Brown developed a special task force that allowed him to appoint members to the school board instead of continuing with the independent election system. In addition, he cast the tie-breaking vote for the city council to pass a similar measure that allowed him to select three of its seven members instead of using the usual election process for all city council seats. Still, seemingly the most divisive part of Brown's new plan for Oakland was his promise to private developers who could no longer afford to build in San Francisco. He assured them quick approval for the development of market-rate apartments and condominiums without the requirement of subsidized and affordable housing. As Brown's promise coincided with the computer technology boom, the average rental cost of an apartment in Oakland increased by 65 percent from 1995 to 2000. For the first time in fifty years the 2000 census showed a significant increase in Oakland's population of white residents (Rhomberg 2004, 188–191). As a result of such an extreme shift in housing costs, many poor black families were forced out. For poor families that remained, already harsh living conditions only worsened. With few opportunities to work and advance in the changing local economy, what I describe as "grinding" in chapter 1 became central to the day-to-day functioning of many residents.

RACE, CLASS, AND GENDER IN THE INNER CITY

Joblessness, welfare dependency, single parenthood, crime, and disorder are all a part of a harsh social and economic environment experienced proportionally more by blacks than by any other racial or ethnic group. These conditions become a part of the daily life of blacks, who are the most spatially isolated population in the United States because of racial segregation and geographically concentrated poverty. The women in this study have all been born and raised in a community shaped by poverty, crime, joblessness, welfare dependency, and single parenthood. Each of these women inhabits a community plagued by these characteristics today. Their experiences are informed not only by structural circumstances but also by intersections of race, gender, and class.

The gendered expectations of women largely reflect white, middle-class understandings of femininity. Race and class complicate these expectations for black women in urban communities. Black notions of respectability and uplift as standards of living are rooted in white, middle-class notions of acceptable behavior and ways of living and being. Community and even individual commitments to such standards of living significantly increase local pressure on young black women regarding the importance of living one's life according to these principles. Further, poverty has been a historical marker of those who are in need of uplift and who need to know the expectations of respectability as a way of life. Yet being a member of the working poor and living in a distressed inner-city community requires that black women "work the code" and employ multiple strategies on a daily basis in an effort to ensure their survival (Jones 2008). At times such work can encourage behaviors that violate traditional mainstream expectations of femininity and as a result may further complicate the daily lived experiences of inner-city girls (Anderson 1999; Collins 2005; Gaines 1996; Higginbotham 1994; Jones 2010).

Girls' experiences are patterned by gender in other ways. For example, Robin D. G. Kelley (1997) describes the gender boundaries placed upon women and girls by caretakers in the inner city. Such boundaries can help fuel the already present situational sense of fear. Often, young women and girls can experience some level of confinement due to traditionally imposed gender roles in cooking, cleaning, childcare, and the like. Additionally, Kelley notes, they are "policed by family members, authorities, and boys themselves from the 'dangers' of the streets." He asserts that "the fear of violence and teen pregnancy has led parents to cloister girls even more" than boys (Kelley 1997, 54–55). In other cases, girls may challenge and break through these restrictive boundaries, thus subjecting the girls to penalties both private and public. As they defy gendered expectations they risk being evaluated as below mainstream and black middle-class expectations of appropriate and respectable femininity. Young women who are assessed in this way are typically seen as less than respectable and in turn less deserving of respect and the special treatment reserved for "good girls." Such evaluations work to complicate their interactions with others, making them vulnerable to microinteractional assaults.

An Overview of the Chapters

In this book I offer an ethnographic account of how black women navigate distressed urban neighborhoods. Respondents in my study described life in East Oakland as "the grind." In chapter 1, I describe the various aspects of the grind, including the intense physical and emotional work required to negotiate the demands of daily life in this inner-city community. In the following chapters, I systematically examine how women manage interactions on the street and within neighborhood establishments such as grocery stores, corner stores, and check-cashing businesses. My analysis reveals that women in this space experience a range of negative encounters that are all complicated by prevailing ideas about gender, race, and class. I analyze these occurrences as cases of microinteractional assaults and dedicate chapters 2 and 3 to explaining how these scenes unfold in public space. First, I explore how hostile encounters unfold in local businesses. I then turn my analysis to a particular kind of street-based microinteractional assault, which is informed by the gendered power dynamics that play out among women and men in public. This type of microinteractional assault is also shaped by the act or threat of sexual violence. In chapter 3, I reveal the situated strategies women use to negotiate these troubling, everyday experiences. In one strategy, which my respondents refer to as "keeping it fresh," women draw on their limited material resources to present themselves in a way that they believe will provide a buffer against microinteractional assaults. Such strategies often work because they effectively draw on the same class, race, and gendered assumptions that inform the episodes themselves. Yet even when these strategies are not successful in changing the ideas and actions of outsiders they remain valuable to women. One outcome of such strategies is making women feel better in a setting where there is little to feel good about. In this book, my original analysis of routine public interactions illustrates the lived experiences of poor black women and the creative strategies they develop to manage these events and survive in a community commonly exposed to violence.

In chapter 1, I describe how black women make money in neighborhoods that are shaped by underemployment, poverty, and racial segregation, and I explain what it means for black women to "grind" in this setting. The grind includes two common ways that women make money: some women adopt a half-time hustle, participating in both low-wage jobs within the formal economy and entrepreneurial ventures in the underground marketplace; others become urban entrepreneurs who take part in paid work within the underground marketplace. All women must contend with the violence that occurs in the neighborhood. In an effort to survive the grind, women rely on extended care networks.

In chapter 2, I define and describe microinteractional assaults, the negative interactional exchanges experienced by some black women when they frequent local businesses. I explain the routine nature of these encounters for black women who live in distressed urban settings, and draw on cases of microassaults in two key social settings: local businesses like the grocery and corner stores, and financial establishments like check-cashing businesses. Finally I explain how the conditions of these different local settings influence these interactions and their consequences in various ways.

In chapter 3, I explore a particular kind of microinteractional assault that occurs on the street. I describe how this type of public interaction is similar and different from those described in chapter 2 and also explore how such an interaction is influenced by poverty as well as racial and class isolation in this setting. Street-based microinteractional assaults are different from the microinteractional assaults described in chapter 2 in that these negative interactional exchanges occur outside the boundaries of local businesses. These encounters are informed by gendered power dynamics and are shaped by the act or threat of sexual violence. I describe the characteristics of this particular type of interaction and explore how dominant controlling images of black women in the inner city influence the nature of these types of scenes as well as the strategies of resistance developed by women in this setting.

In chapter 4, I define and describe the situated strategy of "keeping it fresh," an aesthetic performance that involves maintaining a neat and stylish appearance enhanced by expensive clothes, shoes, and accessories acquired through networks within the local informal economy. I show how black women keep it fresh as a preemptive strategy to buffer themselves from microinteractional assaults. Women in this setting are always accountable to the expectations of what raced and gendered poverty ought to look like, and keeping it fresh works to contradict these prevailing notions. This form of self-presentation aims to discredit any evaluation labeling those who keep it fresh as poor and unworthy of respect, even for a moment. Even when it doesn't work, the act of keeping it fresh is important because women feel good when they look good, and feeling good even for a short time makes daily life just a little easier to manage.

In chapter 5, I consider how the interactions black women experience in poor inner-city neighborhoods uncovers contemporary ideas about who they are and who they are not as poor black women. Coming to know and understand the daily life tasks and pressures that accompany troubled urban life for women in this space has revealed an often undervalued side to inner-city life: the power of creativity, community, and the will to carry on in the face of struggle. In closing, I address what my findings suggest for improving the lives of women in the inner city while keeping central what is at stake for poor black women as they work to meet the demands of daily life under harsh conditions.

CHAPTER 1

"Grinding"

LIVING AND WORKING IN EAST OAKLAND

I SIT ON the front steps of my apartment building around 7:15 on a Thursday morning. I have used this time regularly over the past six months to observe the morning routines of local residents. I wave to Ruth, the nineteen-year-old mother of a two-year-old boy. I look on as she pushes her son's stroller down the street in the direction of where I sit. On many mornings I watch Ruth walk this same path.

"Where you going, Ruth?" I ask with a smile.

She shakes her head and smiles back. "You know where I'm going, taking him to the babysitter, then to King's" (the local fast-food restaurant where she works). She points to the long-sleeved yellow shirt she wears with the restaurant's emblem printed on the front. "I gotta stay on my grind 'cause the bills don't stop."

"Hang in there, and have a good day," I say.

"I'll try," she says over her shoulder, then waves and continues walking.

The grind, or *grinding*, is a term used by black women like Ruth to describe the different types of work they do in distressed urban communities. Ruth walks each day through her troubled inner-city neighborhood as she takes her toddler to a babysitter and then works long hours at King's. Her reference

to "my grind" reveals both the physical and emotional work
required to negotiate the demands of daily life in distressed
inner-city space. For women in this neighborhood, *grinding* is
a term that can refer to work in both the formal and the underground economies. There are four dimensions to grinding for
women in this setting:

> *The half-time hustle:* Participation in both low-wage
> jobs within the formal economy and entrepreneur-
> ial ventures in the underground marketplace.
>
> *Underground entrepreneurship:* Paid work in the under-
> ground marketplace that commonly includes
> selling stolen goods from retail stores out of cars,
> homes, or on the street for a discounted price.
>
> *Managing violence:* Negotiating daily work in the formal
> and informal economy as both become routinely
> complicated by the presence of neighborhood
> violence.
>
> *Surviving the grind:* Coping with the stress and emo-
> tional labor that accompany both low-wage and
> underground labor while working to stay safe in a
> neighborhood regularly exposed to violence.

As a term, *grinding* reflects the intensity and drudgery of managing these dimensions of daily life. Not all women experience
all dimensions at the same time, but among those women I
interviewed it was common to experience underground entre-
preneurship, managing violence, and sometimes more at a given
time. The intersection of physical and emotional labor make
up the grind for women in this setting. The pressure of the
grind is exacerbated by the intense demands of daily life, both
physical and emotional, that these women encounter each day.

How do women overcome the challenges of paying the
bills and caring for their family in settings like East Oakland?

Ruth works at the fast-food restaurant by day and as a seamstress at night and on weekends. Ruth and her retired mother
are unlawfully employed by a dry-cleaning business that pays
them weekly in cash, off the books, and well below minimum
wage to complete store orders requiring sewing or alterations.
Ms. Jenny is a middle-aged woman who works full-time in
the underground marketplace, using space in her home to resell
stolen goods to those who cannot afford to buy those same
goods in retail stores. It is not likely that successfully negotiating the grind will lead to stable careers for Ruth or Ms. Jenny.
Still, the women do this work because they have few other
options to provide for themselves and their families.

I draw on cases discovered during my field research and
interviews to illustrate what the grind looks like from the
perspective of women like Ruth and Ms. Jenny. Respondent
accounts shed light on how structural and cultural circumstances
further shape women's work at low-wage jobs and entrepreneurial ventures in the underground marketplace as a way to make
money. The grind is complicated by the presence of neighborhood violence and the stress and emotional labor required to
stay safe in its presence. This analysis of the grind also reveals
how women manage constraining and contradictory gendered
expectations in this setting.

GRINDING IN EAST OAKLAND:
HUSTLING TO SUPPLEMENT
LOW-WAGE WORK

Douglas S. Massey and Nancy A. Denton argue that "segregation plays a key role in depriving poor black families of access
to goods and services because it interacts with poverty to create
neighborhood conditions that make it nearly impossible to sustain a viable retail sector" (1993, 135). In distressed communities
without a workable retail segment, residents find it nearly impossible to obtain necessary goods and services and become further

excluded from mainstream job opportunities. With such limited possibilities before them, the lives and work of hustlers, drug dealers, and pimps become more attractive and appear to be a route toward success (Anderson 1990).

These changes are obvious in East Oakland; the presence of work within the underground marketplace is largely a result of such depressed employment opportunities and a lack of accessible goods and services. Here residents must go in search of daily necessities because institutionalized racism has prevented such retail establishments from setting up businesses in this community. Not only is racial isolation taking place as a result, but the conditions also produce "profound alienation from American society and its institutions" as a disturbing consequence (Massey and Denton 1993, 160).

In East Oakland, women sometimes turn to work in the underground and illegal economies as a means of economic survival. They engage in a range of what they refer to as "hustles" to make money. Prostitution, drug sales, theft, and credit card, identity, and insurance scams (such as burning down one's own property or arranging for one's property to be "stolen" in order to file a report of arson or theft and claim the insurance money) are common ways people sustain themselves from day to day. This includes hustling to provide food, clothing, shelter, and other basic needs for themselves and their families. Grinding represents the different types of intense work that black women do, including hustling to manage life in troubled inner-city neighborhoods. The grind includes two common ways that women make money: through low-wage work in the formal economy and through paid work in the underground marketplace. Some women adopt a half-time hustle while others become urban entrepreneurs. Women in East Oakland often hold low-wage jobs that require long hours of labor-intensive work, but for many such jobs fail to provide a decent wage. In order to approximate a livable wage some women supplement their income from low-wage paid work with income from hustles worked within the underground marketplace. Such half-time hustles can provide economically vulnerable women with a place to live and food to eat.

The following account from Rachel, a twenty-one-year-old Oakland native, illustrates how she simultaneously works as a nursing assistant and orchestrates insurance fraud to provide basic needs for herself and her developmentally disabled ten-year-old brother, for whom she is the primary caretaker. Rachel's work as a nursing assistant takes place at a resident care facility a short bus ride away from her home. As she explains, "I work a lot and still don't have enough money for everything we need. He [her brother] needs extra stuff that other kids don't, and Social Security only covers some of it. The rest I have to come up with. . . . I have had a few cars stolen and one catch on fire over the last couple of years just so I can get the insurance money. It's not something I'm proud of, but at the time I didn't really see another way."

Although Rachel is lawfully employed full-time, she resorts to insurance fraud just to get by financially. This type of fraud is not uncommon here, as Rachel goes on to tell me that it is from people she knows in the neighborhood that she learned of this scam and how to carry it out. She says that she grinds "all day, everyday," but it is apparent that grinding for her is much more than going to her nursing assistant job. The work that Rachel does both professionally and illegally is an example of one way the hustle is used in conjunction with low-wage paid work.

Ruth, the 19-year old mother of a two-year-old, has lived in East Oakland over half of her young life. She, like Rachel, must also depend on a half-time hustle in order to provide basic needs for herself and her son. Ruth describes the "under-the-table" work she and her retired mother do to provide for their household:

My mom is really good at sewing. She always has been, but never did it full-time because she couldn't ever make enough money at it to quit her other job as a janitor for the school district. But one day she got this chance to sew for this dry-cleaning place. They said they would pay her in cash once a week and drop off and pick up the stuff that needed to be mended. I do the work with her whenever I'm not at my day job. Even though it's a lot of work for not much money it pays in cash, on time, every week. So it's something we can pretty much count on.

Ruth and her mother work together to maintain their part-time hustle. This work is illegal, but it adds significantly to how they provide for their household. Although Ruth works full-time at King's and her mother collects minimal retirement benefits from her janitorial job, the underground seamstress work they do each week is something they have come to rely on just as they do with the legal forms of income they earn. This type of work or "general labor" in both legal and illegal sectors is not uncommon for individuals and families struggling to survive in the inner city (Venkatesh 206, 34). Some legitimate businesses hire individuals on an occasional basis to complete small jobs; these jobs usually pay in cash, do not require employees to have proper certification or training, have no job security, and do not offer health or retirement benefits, workers compensation, and the like. Ruth's mother's weekly tailoring and mending work offers no stability and can be discontinued at any time without notice. For Ruth, grinding consists of both the work she does at her restaurant job and the routine underground seamstress work she and her mother do. Together this part-time hustle and low-wage work make it possible to provide some basic needs for their family.

Vanessa, a twenty-four-year-old mother of eight-month-old twin boys, has worked as an administrative assistant at a local city government agency for the last three years since earning her associate degree in business. Vanessa proudly tells me how she put herself through school to earn her degree, which made getting her job possible. Though currently working in this position full-time, Vanessa also earns money as an unlicensed hairdresser, an underground job she has held since her teens. This part-time hustle is what paid for her education and now supplements the limited income she earns at her day job.

The underground work that women like Vanessa, Ruth, and others take on challenges the stereotypes of poor black women as lazy welfare queens. As Vanessa explains, "I have always liked doing hair and became pretty good at it. My sister went to cosmetology school and taught me a lot of what I know. When I was a kid I was always asking my friends to let me do their hair so I could practice just for fun. Then I got good, and people wanted me to do their hair for real. That is when I realized I could make money doing this. I have been ever since."

Vanessa's part-time hustle as a hairdresser helped her finance her education at the local community college. Without this part-time work she explains that earning her associate degree would not have been possible. Now as an administrative assistant and new mother of twins, her part-time hustle is still a vital financial resource for herself and her family. She explains that her day job provided "just okay" financially for her individually, but now with two children she regularly depends on the money she earns from her half-time hustle to help provide for her family's basic needs. Vanessa's illegal work as an unlicensed hairdresser and professional work as a city government employee operate in conjunction to help her provide for the daily needs of herself and her young children.

For Rachel, Ruth, and Vanessa, part-time hustles are central to the ways in which they manage their daily lives in the inner city. Many working-poor individuals and families in the inner city have come to depend upon underground work, though many do not generally condone illegal behavior and some even fear the dangers associated with illegal hustles (Venkatesh 2006, chap.7). Women like Rachel, Ruth, and Vanessa use low-wage work and illegal hustles as a means of economic survival. Some may participate in illegal work with goals of attaining power, prestige, and social mobility according to local standards, but for the women in this study, low-wage work and half-time hustles are about day-to-day economic survival with the hope of creating some level of economic stability even within this highly unstable underground arena. It is important to note that without significant changes in resources and opportunities for those living in poor urban communities like East Oakland, economic stability and upward mobility remain unlikely but the availability of underground work will persist. The half-time hustle operates in what Sudhir Alladi Venkatesh describes as the "shady world." In this environment, inner-city households depend upon work as well as "off the books transactions" in the underground marketplace (2006, chap. 7).

The unlawful work performed by women in this study reflects the necessity of low-wage work and the half-time hustle working in conjunction as a means of financial survival. For women to maintain their full-time socially legitimate work and support their families it is important to some that their part-time hustles involve less violence and carry lesser legal penalties than hustles involving, for example, the drug trade. In this way the half-time hustle is different from the often gang-affiliated full-time criminal activity illustrated in what Venkatesh describes as "shady dealings" (2006, chap. 7). The types of half-time hustles performed by these women differ somewhat in nature even as the reasons why they participate in such illegal work are similar. Each woman is lawfully employed full-time but still does not earn enough money to consistently provide basic needs for herself and her family. In turn, they all rely on this underground work to supplement the income earned from low-wage work. This dimension of the grind is central to how women and girls negotiate distressed daily life in the inner city.

While some women avoid hustles that increase the threat of violence, some women take part in underground work that heightens their risk of physical violence. In addition to individual strategies like those described above, women and girls are also involved in underground marketplaces like the drug trade. Gender patterns their involvement in these systems in key ways. In general, the underground marketplace in this setting is male dominated; men in their late teens through middle age generally control this underground system while employing women to do work within it as subordinates but not typically as partners. By a large margin men run the "drug game," but they are increasingly recruiting young girls as "runners" for the delivery and pickup of their products and payments. These drug dealers also use young girls as lookouts for police and threatening outsiders. For men, markers such as the number of employees, women, property, cars, jewelry, and clothes they have determine their status. Some exceptions to these rules include traditional and nontraditional family legacies or carrying out crimes "successfully" that have gone unsolved by the police or higher-level public authorities. These exceptions grant limited flexibility upon gaining a "respected" place within the hierarchy, but only consistent successful work—or "putting in work," as some have described it—maintains one's status within it.

Limitations for women and girls in the local drug trade can make hustles like Ms. Jenny's (which I will describe in the next section) and others' seem more appealing. In a male-dominated system Ms. Jenny has developed her own business that attracts regular customers. Her business is centered around the resale of stolen merchandise, but her work doesn't involve the same types of risks that often come with the drug trade. Notably, less violence and lower penalties from law enforcement can attract more women to the underground buying and selling of goods.

HUSTLING IN THE UNDERGROUND MARKETPLACE: THE CASE OF MS. JENNY

One day I notice two children, a boy and a girl, who both look around eight or nine years old. They are dressed in uniforms of black pants and white polo-style shirts. Looking on, I see the two children pass the driveway of Ms. Jenny's home. A black woman in her fifties, Ms. Jenny stands on her small porch in a housedress as she directs two young men carrying goods into her home. The young men make three trips between their minivan and Ms. Jenny's front door, carrying several shoeboxes and overstuffed garment bags. I have seen these same young men make deliveries to Ms. Jenny around this time before. I have also observed many local residents come and go from Miss Jenny's home carrying clothes, shoes, and a variety of other goods. Ms. Jenny is what I refer to as an underground entrepreneur: a person who sells stolen goods from retail stores out of their cars, homes, or on the street for a discounted price.

I first met Ms. Jenny through my neighbor Ms. Loretta, a retired postal worker in her late fifties. After talking informally on several occasions about both my field of study and happenings in the neighborhood, she tells me that she and Ms. Jenny have been friends for several years. I ask her to introduce me to Ms. Jenny and she agrees. On a Saturday afternoon in October Ms. Loretta and I begin the short walk from our apartment complex to Ms. Jenny's home. When we reach the modest single family home, I follow Ms. Loretta up three steps to the front porch and she rings the doorbell. I see a pair of eyes quickly pull back the curtain of a small window positioned on the left side of the front door.

"Is that you, Loretta?" I hear a woman say in a friendly voice as she unlocks the several deadbolts on her front door.

"Hey Jenny," Ms. Loretta replies with a smile as the front door of the home swings open.

"Who is that?" Ms. Jenny says with a frown as she sees me standing beside her friend.

"Remember the girl I told you about who is doing a project for school?"

"Oh yeah, I sure do. Nice to meet you baby, come on in." Ms. Jenny ushers us in her front door.

Inside Ms. Jenny's home I follow her and Ms. Loretta into the "store," as Ms. Jenny calls it, a two-room extension that was added on to the back of the house. The first thing I notice upon entering the brightly lit room is a wall safe resembling those designed to hold rifles and other artillery, wide enough for me to walk inside and reaching from floor to ceiling. Ms. Jenny watches closely as Ms. Loretta and I look at her merchandise, neatly organized by item type. I see clothing, shoes, and accessories of all styles, colors, and sizes arranged on display tables and hanging on wardrobe racks. Ms. Jenny asks for my help to reach a box on a high shelf; it contains goods pre-ordered by Ms. Loretta. After I retrieve the box for her she begins to remove its contents, a variety of children's clothing items. She holds up each item, including jeans, shirts, dresses, and coats, and hands it to Ms. Loretta to review before putting it back in the box. Happy with her order, Ms. Loretta hands Ms. Jenny a white envelope. Ms. Jenny opens and quickly examines its contents with her fingers. Seemingly satisfied, with a smile on her round face, she folds the envelope and places it into the pocket of her housedress. She turns and asks me, "Is there any-thing you want to take a closer look at?"

"Not today, but can I come back and look around?"

"Sure, and remember if there is something you want in a magazine or in a catalog, just bring me the picture and I can get it for you."

"Okay," I say, then ask, "Would you be willing to talk with me a little about your work sometime?"

"If you come back with an order and make a decent pur-chase I will gladly answer your questions," she says with a laugh. "Business is business, baby."

"Okay, Ms. Jenny, I understand. You got a deal."

"Let Loretta know when you're ready to come back and she will call me and then we can go from there."

"All right, I will," I reply as Ms. Jenny escorts us to the front door.

After meeting Ms. Jenny I followed up with her and returned to her "store" and purchased a pair of blue jeans and a plain black sweater. After I had made the purchase, Ms. Jenny seemed a little more relaxed in my presence and agreed to talk with me. I followed Ms. Jenny through her small kitchen and to a door that led to her well-manicured backyard. We each sat on overturned milk crates and leaned against the back wall of the house as she struggled with the slight breeze to light her cigarette. After taking a long drag on it, Ms. Jenny began explaining to me some of the challenges she has faced operat-ing her underground business full-time for the last eight years. She has been robbed twice—"which isn't bad," she says—and has had some "issues" with law enforcement regard-ing her goods that she would not elaborate on when I asked her if she could tell me more about it. She tells of the "good" she has done through her business: helping women and men look their best for job interviews, dressing kids for their high school proms and graduations, and supplying families with cribs, clothes, and diapers as they prepare for the arrival of a new baby.

"Do they pay you for this stuff?" I ask.

"Well, yeah—nothing is free. I have given things away before, but I need to keep a roof over my head too. I'm not saying I'm a saint, but I help a lot of people look good and feel their best through my business. They probably wouldn't have nearly as nice quality of shoes and clothes and things if I didn't run my business here. I do what I can."

The full-time work that Ms. Jenny does in the underground marketplace is largely a result of her being laid off from her janitorial job of twenty-three years. She explained to me how she had always sold clothes and shoes here and there and around holidays when she came across a good supplier. I listen as she describes using this money to pay for unexpected expenses like medical bills when her children would get sick and getting her car repaired when it would break down. Yet after losing the janitorial job she had worked at for half her lifetime she was forced to sell stolen goods full-time. "I kept getting turned down from other cleaning jobs 'cause they can get young people to do the same work twice as fast, so I had to do something else," she explains. This is when Ms. Jenny began to turn her seasonal hustle into a full-time underground business of sorts. She focused on building her business while staying beneath the radar of law enforcement as best she could. "Selling clothes and things has given me a way to pay my bills and help my kids from time to time. It's not easy, and it has risks, but I truly don't know how I would have made it otherwise." Ms. Jenny had worked tirelessly at a paid low-wage job for over two decades, but at the time when many consider retirement she was unexpectedly laid off, and she was forced to find other work to keep "a roof over her head"—risky and illegal work in the underground marketplace.

NEGOTIATING NEIGHBORHOOD
VIOLENCE

Women like Ms. Jenny grind against a backdrop of violence
that poor inner-city residents are routinely exposed to. Even
though much of the violence involves men in and outside the
community, women like Ruth and Ms. Jenny are also affected
as witnesses to the violence that takes place. Women in the community are also connected to experiences of violence through
their relationships to men and boys. Such encounters can threaten
their safety and that of their family, depending upon how they
react to what they have witnessed and with whom they choose
to discuss it. In addition to their experiences as bystanders, there
is the very real issue of men involved in crimes thinking that a
woman who was hanging around when something went down
"couldn't keep her mouth shut." Whether the woman talked to
the police, a friend, or neither one, if there is even the slightest
assumption that she "ran her mouth," death, physical assault,
and/or sexual assault could be a real possibility for her and her
family. Monique, a twenty-four-year-old East Oakland resident,
explains a violent experience regarding snitching that still
haunts her:

> My friend Sasha was walking home one night and saw this
> car creeping down the street with its headlights off. She
> ran behind a Dumpster hoping they hadn't seen her because
> she knew they were probably about to shoot at somebody
> and she didn't want to see or hear anything. A week or so
> later the guy who was shot that night died in the hospital.
> My homegirl [Sasha] said she didn't talk to anybody or say
> anything about being out that night, but it didn't matter.
> A couple of days after the man died in the hospital, two
> guys rolled up on Sasha as she was walking home. They

grabbed her in the middle of the day and beat her up bad, right on the street, near where she was on the night of the shooting. They left her on the sidewalk, bleeding and barely conscious. All that happened, and she didn't snitch on anybody. The crazy thing is it doesn't really matter if she did or not; they were going to make sure she would be too scared to even think about snitching on anyone about anything, ever.

In this way young women are held to the same "no snitching" standards as others in the community. To "not snitch" or to not "be a snitch" requires that those who live here do not discuss what goes on with outsiders. "No snitching" is an unwritten rule of the street that one should not cross or ignore. The rule applies to any and all people who live in the community, and the code also has very racialized and gendered aspects. Black women are not to snitch on black men; they must remain silent not only out of fear of retaliation but also out of loyalty and a sense of community—spatially and in terms of racial solidarity. This takes place in opposition to outsiders—primarily, law enforcement.

The following field note entry illustrates a black woman's allegiance to the community expectation of not snitching as well as how local law enforcement perceives this commitment as loyalty to local criminals. The field note entry documents an encounter that occurred when police in this East Oakland community barricaded an entire neighborhood block while questioning residents in an effort to find suspects in a robbery at a local takeout restaurant:

On a Friday night around 11:30 p.m., I am on my way home. I approach the street I live on and see that a barricade of police cars restricts it. I drive around to the other end of the block and see that no entrance is allowed there either. I park my car on a side street and walk up to one of the six white male officers standing around. They look to be doing nothing in particular. I ask one of the officers what is going on. "Nothing out of the ordinary," he replies, giving a slight chuckle. I do not laugh. He sees that I'm not laughing goes on to explain that Lucky Pond, a Chinese takeout restaurant a block away, was robbed. He says, "This is the third in a string of restaurant robberies over the last two weeks. The suspects held the place up with shotguns and then took off on foot." They ran behind the restaurant and are suspected to be hiding in one of the houses on this block. The officer goes on to say that he and the other officers "had gone door-to-door searching with no luck, really only because no one on this street would give up the suspects. Of course, no one knows anything, as usual. The woman in the house over there"—he points off into the distance—"just stared at us when she finally opened her door. We repeatedly asked her questions, but she just stood there."

Though I know exactly what he is referring to, I ask the officer, "What do you mean 'as usual'?"

"You know," he says, "the people over here and in other neighborhoods around here, too, never *know anything*. They would rather live with these criminals than tell us where they are so we can lock them up."

Outsiders are often frustrated by the silence described by this officer. If people don't "give up" suspects, then it is the residents who are seen as partially responsible for the crime and violence. According to this officer, the woman questioned by the police at her doorstep simply replied to the questions asked of her with a blank stare. The officer's comments suggest that he did not expect anything more from this woman or any other resident. The officer, though still an outsider to this space, knew of the "code" of silence at work. For residents like the woman he sought to question, this silence makes sense. In the earlier account given by Monique she describes how her friend Sasha was brutally beaten in broad daylight by two men. The woman's attack was linked to her presence near the scene of a drive-by shooting. On the night of the crime Sasha hid, yet the violence later directed toward her at this site indicates that she was in fact detected on the night the shooting occurred. Once the shooting victim was pronounced dead, the urgency of silencing any and all potential witnesses seemed to become critical for those involved. Soon after the case was elevated to a homicide, Sasha, a potential witness, was approached by two unknown men and viciously beaten. Cases like this one not only traumatize the victim but work to frighten others and remind them of the dangerous costs that can come with snitching, the perception of being a snitch, or just being in the wrong place at the wrong time. Violence like this targeted at innocent people can prompt blank stares and long silences when local residents are questioned by law enforcement regarding crimes and those involved.

When police officers questioned residents while looking for suspects in the robbery of the takeout restaurant they described blank stares and silence as a means by which neighborhood residents protect criminals. The police officers see these types of responses to questioning as adherence to criminality. In turn, local residents are trying to stay safe in a place where violent attacks can be waged based on the possibility of someone snitching. Responding to officers with silence and blank stares appears to be a way that some women stay safe. Women like Monique and Sasha are particularly vulnerable to the potential punishments that come with living in a neighborhood plagued by violence, poverty, and social isolation. Such punishments include intense acts of violence and persistent crime. The lack of cooperation with police here seems to be in part based on trying to ensure one's own safety, not an effort to protect criminal behavior. In the end, it is safer to maintain and respect the "code" of this community than to risk intervention at the hands of outsiders, even if they are paid to patrol and protect (Anderson 1999).

Violence and Routine Activities

Like their male counterparts, women and girls live in an East Oakland community that is shaped by poverty, underemployment, joblessness, and violence. Such elements affect residents both socially and psychologically. One result of the changes these neighborhoods have experienced over time is the exposure to lethal violence. Elijah Anderson (1999) shows that when unemployment, poor public services, racism, crime, and hopelessness are present within distressed urban neighborhoods, violence and other aggressive behavior often persist. The lives of residents who exist within the confines of such circumstances are affected directly in myriad ways. The following excerpt from my field notes illustrates how the threat of violence influences the most routine of activities in this setting.

> It's late Friday afternoon; the sun is blazing on this July day. The voice on the radio blasting from a neighboring apartment, just steps away from the one I share with my mother, says between songs that the temperature is 89 degrees right now. Most of the neighborhood sits outside under trees and in any other spare patches of shade (no one I know of here has air-conditioning). Music blares from parked cars as young men and boys walk by without shirts, women and girls in shorts and short dresses, and babies walk around wearing only diapers. The feeling outside is tense, as is usual with such high temperatures—which also signal trouble. I sit on the curb with a neighbor as she and I talk and watch her children play before us. Slowly a neon orange "scraper" on wheel rims that look to

be at least 24s [twenty-four inches in diameter] drives down the street at a respectful pace considering a lot of kids are at play in and out of the street. Everyone I notice looks up as the car passes by.

On hot days such as this it is very common to see scrapers joyriding. A scraper is a sedan, usually a late 1980s to early 1990s American car, often a Buick, Chevrolet, or Dodge. It is commonly painted a neon color, with tinted windows and very large wheel rims, no less than twenty-two inches in diameter. Scrapers became very popular with the rise of the Oakland area hyphy movement and the associated cultural performance known as ghost riding. On hot days when many people are outside, car owners commonly joyride and show off their scrapers for others to admire, similar to an auto show. Yet, with this show comes some apprehensions. Because many people do hang outside in order to escape the heat, this has also proven to be an easier time to settle prior debts via drive-by shootings. In this neighborhood, such gun violence is not unusual. Each time a scraper that has been associated with drive-by gun violence comes down a street at a slower than usual pace it could mean one of two things: the driver is taking caution for children at play or possible gun violence is about to occur. Tensions rise and fall continuously through the community at the thought of the latter.

Children and adults alike spend time this afternoon outside their homes trying to get some relief from the sweltering heat overtaking the space indoors. As adults make conversation with friends and neighbors and children play the feeling here seems peaceful. This mood changes within moments at the sight of a neon scraper slowly driving down the street. Most of the chatter stops as parents begin to look around and locate their children and people begin to move out of the street. I notice a few people move some distance away from the side-walk toward residences. The sudden change in tone among individuals and families cooling off outside their homes on this afternoon is an example of how violence and the threat of violence influences even the most routine activities.

A central component of the intensity of the grind is developing strategies to manage violence. Yet violence works to further complicate the emotional labor, low-wage work, and work in the underground marketplace that represent the intense struggle required for women to make money here. In this case, the threat of violence disrupts how local residents are managing a routine activity—staying cool on a hot day. Some retreat to their homes, which are likely uncomfortable places to be on a day like this; yet with no place else to go and the risk of violence taking place just outside their door, many are left with few options. Observing how violence can and often does upset routine activities underscores how it can easily make the grind harder than it already is.

Managing the Threat of Violence

In an effort to manage, survive, and operate in this environment and its culture, residents must become familiar with the "code of the street," a "set of informal rules governing interpersonal public behavior, particularly violence" (Anderson 1999, 33, 109). It is through this code that public social behavior is organized and often governed. The foundation of the "code" is respect, and without respect, either given or received, penalties are imposed (Anderson 1999). Nikki Jones (2010) writes that the "code" is not gender specific. As a means of survival in the inner-city community "young women . . . are encouraged to embrace some aspects of the 'code of the street'" (Jones 2008, 76; see also Anderson 1999). Anderson's concept of the "code of the street" emphasizes the alienation and isolation that has resulted from the changing face of urban communities across the United States and the culture of these neighborhoods over the last several decades. Changing social norms, the lack of economic opportunities, and the increasingly harsh conditions of urban life have encouraged new ways of operating for the people who are confined to live in these spaces.

People develop a range of strategies to navigate this setting. In Jones's study of African American adolescent girls and inner-city violence, she discusses the use of *situated survival strategies* as "patterned forms of interpersonal interaction, and routine or ritualized activities oriented around a concern for securing their personal well-being" (2010, 52–53). Such behaviors include, but are not limited to, fighting and other forms of physical aggression usually associated with boys and masculinity. The situated survival strategies employed by these young girls represent an effort to "effectively manage potential threats of interpersonal violence . . . at the risk of violating mainstream and local expectations regarding appropriate feminine behavior" (Jones 2010, 9).

Jones presents two strategies in her study. The first is *situational avoidance*, which encapsulates all of the effort and labor that inner-city adolescent girls undertake in order to avoid situations that could prove to be potentially threatening to their well-being and to avoid sites at which conflict might easily arise. The conscious and routine avoidance of probable circumstances and places of conflict is necessary in order to ensure safety in distressed urban communities. The second strategy, *relational isolation*, uncovers the consistent and deliberate effort to isolate oneself from building friendships and other close relationships in an attempt to avoid possible future situations of conflict directed at friends of loved ones that may require their involvement defensively. All of this takes place within the context of mainstream gendered expectations, accountability, and beliefs regarding femininity and the ways in which girls—particularly black girls—"should" behave in their daily lives in the inner city (Jones 2010, chap. 2).

In the following account, Amber, a nineteen-year-old expectant mother, describes how she must regulate where she goes and who she spends time with to try and stay safe while living in the neighborhood:

> My grandfather used to always say, "Pay attention wherever and whenever because you never know when somebody might get crazy." I know now that he was right. I always switch up the way I walk to the bus stop and to work or wherever I have to go. I never go the same way two days in a row 'cause I don't want anybody to pick up my pattern and surprise me one day. I also hang with the same girls. Me and my two best friends have been cool since we were in the second grade. We grew up together and we been through a lot with each other: boys, fights, babies, all kinds of stuff, so we cool. I sometimes hang out with a couple of the girls from work who are okay, but I never bring them over here [to her neighborhood]; we not tight like that. I also don't mess with no dudes that's trying to hustle hard [sell drugs]. My ex-boyfriend is in jail now because of drugs. When I was with him it was this one time that we were at this hamburger place where you stand outside and order through a window and it was late, about eleven or eleven thirty p.m., and these two guys rolled up and we were so busy looking at the menu we didn't see these two guys about to rush us. One of the guys choked me out and the other one held his pistol to my boyfriend's head until he gave him all the money he had on him. He had just came from a run so he was carrying about four stacks [four thousand dollars]. It was never the same after that. I

was always scared for us to go out after that. That was the last time I was with somebody who sold drugs like that.

Amber describes here some of the lengths she goes to trying to stay safe. She emphasizes having to walk different routes each day as she travels through the community. In addition to living in a troubled environment this daily task simply adds to the stress involved with living and traveling through this space, further complicating the grind for women here. Amber monitors her movements in the neighborhood to try and avoid being followed or surprised by someone watching her route. She also appears to take pride in the close relationship she has with her two best friends. These relationships seem to offer a level of support to Amber in a place where it is not always clear who is there to help and who is not. She goes on to explain a violent encounter she experienced with her ex-boyfriend as they were picking up a late-night meal when two men surprised them on the street. This encounter helped to shape the kinds of men Amber will or will not associate with; after this encounter she was traumatized to the point that she decided to no longer date men who are involved with selling drugs.[1] She illustrates how violence influences some of the most routine activities that are a part of managing her day-to-day life. Violence and the threat of violence intensify the grind for Amber and others like her in this community everyday.

SURVIVING THE GRIND: THE ROLE OF INFORMAL NETWORKS

At times the work of the grind can be an individual project, but some of the labor of carrying the burden of the grind is a group effort. In addition to their involvement in the underground economy, women also play a large role in maintaining and reproducing a neighborhood social support network that is generally closed to outsiders. This informal network consists of nonfamily members who live in close proximity to one another but not in the same household (Roschelle 1997, 33–34). These members have frequent to semifrequent interaction with neighbors when providing and/or receiving services such as childcare, transportation, food, and household chores as well as sharing ongoing emotional support. Sometimes these services are given in exchange for other goods or services, but not always. I participated in this type of informal social support network when living in the neighborhood and conducting my fieldwork. For example, early one weekday morning Leslie—a twenty-three-year-old mother of a sixteen-month-old daughter, who lived in the unit next door to me—was sitting on the ground in the empty parking stall where her car was usually parked. Dressed in a red polo-style shirt and black pants—the uniform for the office supply store where she worked—she sat shaking her head, looking to be on the verge of tears.

"Everything okay, Leslie?" I asked as I descended the last few steps leading to where she sat.

"No," she cried, "I just got down here and my car is gone."

"Gone?"

"Yeah, like disappeared, stolen—*gone*. I just don't know what to do, 'cause I have to be at work in thirty minutes and I can't be late 'cause I'm on probation, I just got this job and I can't lose it. I am so frustrated I could scream." Tears rolled down her cheeks.

"Come on, I'll take you."

"Huh?" She looked slightly puzzled.

"I'll take you. You said you have to be there on time to keep your job, right?"

"Yeah," she replied, wiping away tears from her face.

"Then let's go."

"Thank you. I owe you, like, for real."

After this occasion, Leslie's usually dry personality began to brighten up when we crossed paths in our complex and around the neighborhood. She began to say hello with a smile and she would regularly introduce me to her friends and relatives as "college girl." About a month or so after I gave Leslie a ride to work she knocked on my door.

"Hey, Leslie," I said as I unlocked my security gate.

"Hey, college girl," she said. "These are for you." She handed me a stack of four composition notebooks and a package of pens. "I see you always writing in these, and I wanted to tell you thank you for taking me to work that day. If I would have been late that day, I would have got fired."

"It was no problem, really—and thank you for the notebooks and pens," I answered.

"But, for real, you're cool. If there is anything I can do for you just let me know. I got you," she said as she walked away.

As Leslie and I began to talk more frequently, sometimes she would ask me to babysit her daughter for short periods of time when her work schedule would overlap with the times her mother or the baby's father were scheduled to come pick up her child. I often agreed. In return, Leslie would regularly offer to help me find participants for my study and would often bring me notebooks, pens, and pencils that she explained she got for a "super discount" at her job.

Yet this support network was not just something between Leslie and me. Ms. Virginia, an older woman who lived on the first floor of the apartment complex where Leslie and I lived, rarely had visitors to come by and check on her, and she was sometimes ill. Tenants in the complex took Ms. Virginia on as their own kin, and she seemed to do the same. One afternoon When I was taking out my garbage I saw Ms. Virginia struggling to get down the stairway while trying to hold onto the railing with one hand and carry her garbage bag in the other.

"Let me take that out for you, Ms. Virginia" I said.

"Oh thank you, baby. That would be a big help to me," She replied.

After taking both bags to the Dumpster, I saw Ms. Virginia making her way back to her apartment.

"Ms. Virginia, you know what?" I said as she turned to look at me. "I really don't mind taking your garbage out for you. If you want, you can just leave your garbage bag outside of your door and I will swing by and take it out when I am coming or going each day."

"Only if it's not too inconvenient," she answered.

"It is no trouble at all; I pass your door everyday."

"Well, I guess I will take you up on that. Thank you."

I noticed Leslie picking up Ms. Virginia's mail and newspaper and placing it by her door many evenings as she would come home from work. On a few occasions I also encountered Ms. Virginia leaving our complex with Tanya, another neighbor in our building, and returning with groceries. Many neighbors seemed to support Ms. Virginia in the ways that they could knowing that she was older—in her seventies, living alone, and appearing to have few friends, relatives, or other resources to aid in her care.

Another member of this social support network in our apartment complex was Robert, a tall slender man in his early forties who was always friendly and wearing a smile. Robert, who worked in construction, became the guardian of his six-year-old niece and eight-year-old nephew when their parents, his sister and brother-in-law, were killed in an auto accident. One evening when I was came by Ms. Virginia's door to take out her trash, she opened her security gate and asked me to come in for a moment. Inside, she briefly explained to me that Robert had been laid off from his job and she had prepared a meal for him and his niece and nephew. She asked me if I could take the dinner she had prepared to Robert's apartment. She also asked me to tell Robert that for as long as he wanted she would be happy to prepare bag lunches for his niece and nephew to take to school. I agreed and delivered the dinner to

Robert's apartment and relayed Ms. Virginia's message to him. The next day I decided to support Robert and his family in a way that I could: on my way home from the local grocery store I left some loaves of bread and bags of apples on Robert's doorstep. Two large bags were already sitting next to his front door, one of which appeared to be oranges and the other potatoes.

The mutual aid performed by those in this social network (including Leslie, Ms. Virginia, Robert, Tanya, myself, and others in the neighborhood) operated as a form of social support. Structurally these informal networks are about purposefully sharing resources as a survival strategy in an attempt to ease economic deficiency (Roschelle 1997, 65). Yet it is important to note that such compensation for social support was not predetermined or required but was often given voluntarily to make life easier for individuals and families who were experiencing particularly hard times. For example, when I gave Leslie a ride to work when her car was stolen and later babysat her daughter, she in turn helped me find participants for my study by asking her friends and relatives if they would be willing to talk to me. She also brought me composition books and pens. These were all ways of offering me social support for the support I had shown her. I did not have a set of expectations for what I would receive or that I would receive anything at all for the aid I had offered Leslie, just as she didn't initially expect me to offer to give her a ride to work the morning her car was stolen. Yet once I initiated an offer of support to her she quickly responded with letting me know that she now felt that she "owed me." I observed no agreed-upon expectations regarding mutual aid, its value, or how it should be compensated, but once someone began performing this work for a neighbor the recipient generally understood that she now "should" repay the other person in some way that was valuable to them. For example, in thanks for the support given to her, Ms. Virginia often gave baked goods or other prepared food items in return. I often came home to notes on my door from her asking me to come by her apartment and pick up a cake, pie, lasagna, or some other dish she had made for me. I observed her often do the same for Leslie and others in our complex. When Robert was hired by another construction company and reported being "back on his feet again," I repeatedly encountered he and Ms. Virginia at the local grocery store and she often spoke of how appreciative she was that he had driven her there or to other places she needed to go.

The exchange of goods and services as a form of social support is surely relied on by some but seemingly appreciated by all. Specifically, this network of support helps make day-to-day life in a troubled environment a bit easier to bear. Amid neighborhood violence, limited local resources, and unstable job prospects, being able to rely on neighbors for support is vital. The mutual trust among neighbors, including a willingness to support one another, reflects Robert J. Sampson, Steven W. Raudenbush, and Felton Earls's (1998) description of "collective efficacy." The presence of such community cohesion challenges prevailing notions that outcomes such as crime and violence are the only results of urban communities plagued by poverty, joblessness, and the like. Providing occasional transportation, gifts of food, help with household chores, and other goods and services to one another illustrates a shared sense of understanding and community among residents within the distressed inner-city space. The continued operation of this non-kin network uncovers some of the struggles that residents face and how they are often forced to rely on one another to manage those struggles. This informal network also operates as a resource for residents who cannot or do not receive a necessary level of support for their daily survival from social services or other community agencies charged with helping families and individuals in distress. Without this independent network, residents who have become more than neighbors to one another and more like family may not survive.

The Boundaries of Social Support

Venkatesh's (2006) study of the underground economy of the urban poor describes a kind of community network that operates between kin and non-kin in an urban setting. Venkatesh sheds light on how poor individuals and families open their homes and what limited resources they have to friends and family who have fallen on hard times. This community network reflects what Carol Stack describes as "domestic networks" (1974, chap. 3), which are established among kin and non-kin as a survival strategy to ease the harsh effects of economic deprivation. Such networks depict a type of exchange relationship rather than a form of collective efficacy. The work performed in these types of networks have clear expectations for reciprocity. Venkatesh explains that it is common for neighbors and friends to "pool together income from various sources, barter for goods, and develop intricate schemes to exchange services" (Venkatesh 2006, 23). Unlike the social support network I describe, there seems to be a lack of mutual trust and desire to support the common good of those within the network without the expectation of being compensated for performing good deeds for one another. As a result, such networks become a sort of exchange relationship rather than just a form of social support. Nevertheless, in many poor communities resources are few and thus many have little to give to others, making reciprocity understood and expected. Yet, as my respondents show in some inner-city settings, there is a strong commitment to community cohesion despite individual struggle for economic survival. This sense of loyalty, mutual trust, and empathy built among neighbors and expressed through an informal social network represents an emotional reaction to the neighborhood as well as the people and institutions of which it is composed (Small 2004, 165, 182; see also Gregory 1998 and Venkatesh 2000).

While participants in the present study show a commitment to their neighbors through acts of social support and through displays of loyalty, mutual trust, and empathy, these acts are unlikely to be solely altruistic all of the time. Reciprocity is not required, but it is understood and expected. Mutuality works to strengthen ties between individuals by operating as a tangible form of one person's appreciation of another's good deed. Reciprocation also works as a way of maintaining balance between neighbors for the generous actions performed versus those received. The boundaries of expectation for reciprocity are carefully maintained by the degree of the act of kindness displayed. In other words, people generally do not give more than they receive. This helps to prevent an altruistic act from descending into exploitation.

Participation in informal social support networks illustrates a way in which social capital is used within this poor community. Mario Luis Small suggests that there are key individual-level factors that contribute to positive outcomes that result from the relationship between the negative condition of neighborhood poverty and social capital; such factors include affect toward one's neighborhood, employment status, age, immigration status, and individual perception of the neighborhood (Small 2004, chap. 8). I propose that the informal social support network found among Leslie, Ms. Virginia, Robert, Tanya, and myself reflects a cross between collective efficacy, domestic networks, and how individuals use social capital. This network is not specifically an exchange relationship but rather an informal commitment to helping those in need in whatever way one can. To belong to the network or to receive support from those involved, reciprocity is appreciated but not required. This network is made up of non-kin ranging in age from their early twenties through mid-seventies who share a level of dedication to supporting those in their immediate surroundings and building a sense of community through social support. This network is fostered out of the common experience of managing impoverished inner-city life and is designed to help ease the strain associated with the daily demands of living under distressed conditions.

With the increasing presence of violence and dwindling mainstream services and professional resources, life is even harder now than it was in previous decades. Today there are fewer stable job opportunities that pay a livable wage, and there is a steady increase in the displacement of poor inner-city residents. Complicated by routine neighborhood violence and a steady decline in local residents' trust in law enforcement require individuals and families to call on others in the community for support. This social support can help supplement some of the work women do to manage their daily involvement in the grind.

A CENTRAL PART of negotiating distressed inner-city life for black women includes the intense formal and informal daily work commonly referred to as the grind. For many women living in this setting, work within the socially legitimate workforce as well as the underground marketplace is often performed to maintain day-to-day survival. The ways in which gender patterns women's involvement in the grind is significant. The majority of respondents in this study are mothers, many of whom are the primary or sole providers for their children. This responsibility has proven to be particularly challenging for mothers living under harsh conditions, including poverty and underemployment. In turn, many women here participate in half-time hustles and the underground marketplace in addition to maintaining low-wage work, all to provide for the daily needs of their families. In the male-dominated underground setting, women and girls are often employed but do not control most aspects of this system, including the "drug game." Those women and girls who do work in the drug trade often work as "runners" or lookouts. This work can carry harsh legal penalties as well as dangerous consequences on the street. Such punishments can discourage the participation of some women in the drug trade and make other types of half-time hustles seem more appealing, something that may be of particular importance to mothers.

Becoming an underground entrepreneur like Ms. Jenny or working as an unlicensed hairdresser like Vanessa or as an "under the table" seamstress like Ruth can offer women a way to make money to help support their families. In addition, the active role of women working in this underground marketplace (particularly as entrepreneurs, like Ms. Jenny) illuminates the changing roles of women in such a male-dominated space. Ms. Jenny's work challenges the common role of women working secondary to men and sheds light on the possibility of upward mobility for women in this system. The consistent participation of women like Vanessa and Ruth who work both underground and in socially legitimate spaces represents a more fluid role that women have developed as they travel in and out of this underground system from day to day.

Structural factors like unemployment, racial segregation, and crime are responsible for the continuation of black poverty in the United States. The segregation that creates communities like East Oakland also creates race and class isolation. Segregation is central to keeping out a workable retail sector in this setting. The grind emerges as a way for black women to make sense of the formal and informal work they do under these conditions.

As a result, underground and often illegal networks have developed to provide necessary goods and services. Working in the underground marketplace is not an easy task for women who are seen as subordinates in this system. As a way of managing survival amid these harsh structural conditions, community members have created their own social support networks that operate as a way to help sustain local families. In chapter 2, I will discuss another demand of life in this setting for black women: I will explore how they manage exposure to microinteractional assaults in their neighborhood, another part of their everyday experience in the grind.

CHAPTER 2

"It Happens All the Time"

DAY-TO-DAY EXPERIENCES WITH MICROINTERACTIONAL ASSAULTS

MANY PEOPLE GIVE little thought to the minor tasks—like going to the bank, buying groceries, or picking up a takeout meal—that help keep their daily lives running smoothly. These errands are just things that must get done. Yet depending upon a person's social class position, she may or may not have a car to load groceries into or a bank account through which to process transactions. Understanding class as a social process means recognizing how it organizes in very direct ways daily demands on both individuals and families. Seeing how social structures of class build frameworks for everyday life and work sheds light on the varied experiences of poor people versus the nonpoor. Attention to many of life's daily tasks is necessary for some and voluntary for others depending on one's social class status. It is the conditions under which demands of daily life occur that are largely determined by class-based resources or the lack thereof.

Social class and social location, in addition to race and gender, largely impact how we experience these types of daily tasks. In particular, living in a poor inner-city community directly informs how one's daily errands unfold (DeVault 1994, 168–169). For example, being an apartment dweller in a low-income neighborhood may require lengthy and routine walks to a laundromat in lieu of on-site laundry facilities often found in apartment complexes in middle-class communities. The simple luxuries of a privileged class status are often taken for granted as we move through our daily routine. When you don't have a car or a bank account and live in a poor urban community, this routine, unfolds in public and, at times, can become humiliating and painful, especially when interacting with others who treat them in harsh and degrading ways. In such cases, women must learn to negotiate what I term the *microinteractional assault*: a particular type of troubled face-to-face public encounter. The general message sent by microinteractional assaults is to intimidate, threaten, instill feelings of inferiority, and make the targeted person feel unwanted and unsafe (Sue 2010, chap. 2).

Few studies acknowledge the microinteractional work that goes into managing public space for black women. This chapter responds to three key questions: What are the central features of a consumer-oriented microinteractional assault? In what ways does this type of interaction typically unfold? What is at stake for these women as they routinely negotiate this kind of interaction? The cases included in this chapter reveal how microinteractional assaults unfold in local community institutions like the grocery store or corner market. An analysis of these cases reveals how inequalities are reproduced in public space during the course of interaction (West and Fenstermaker 2002, chap. 8). In her study on gender and public harassment, Carol Brooks Gardener (1995) emphasizes the significance of encounters in public space, in part due to their frequency and cumulative impact, and particularly on persons who are situationally disadvantaged like women, persons with disabilities, and people of color, among others. Gardener's work illustrates how members of such groups are often excluded from the rules of public courtesy and how that informs their ongoing experiences in public. When a grocery store clerk treats a woman as if she is not deserving of respect, and the woman reacts in a way that unintentionally reinforces this perception, this maintains the basis for the clerk's behavior and his beliefs in the inferiority of black women.

MICROINTERACTIONAL ASSAULTS: A DEFINITION

Microinteractional assaults (MIAs) are a type of troubled public interaction. These encounters reflect and reinforce the social power dynamics among local business owners, employees, and the black women who live in the neighborhood and frequent these businesses. Such assaults can occur during the regular activities required to manage daily life, including buying groceries, cashing checks, and riding the city bus. In East Oakland, women shared with me their experiences with these types of hostile encounters. Terri shared her experience about shopping in a local grocery store: "When I got to the front of the line, I said hello to the checker, and as usual he didn't say anything. I knew from there that it was all downhill. I then see the bagger pretty much throwing my stuff into the bag. When I got home two of my cans were dented. I hate going to that store, but it's the only halfway decent thing over here."

Terri's account displays the routine nature of rude encounters with store personnel, and going to the store thus brings up a range of negative emotions. Her experience contrasts with general public customer service etiquette and basic expectations that many human beings bring to an encounter. Terri perceives that the store employee in this interaction has determined that she is undeserving of common courtesy because of who she is. In general, conversations are expected to be a continued exchange between participants. This includes offering a greeting or invitation with the expectation of receiving a greeting or other form of acknowledgment in return. Terri's greeting to a store employee is met with silence, which is a type of dismissal and a form of rejection. This response suggests that a person is unworthy of the rules of public courtesy and civility. Once customers experience such dismissal on the part of store employees they are simultaneously denied any form of civil customer service. As illustrated in other cases presented later in the chapter, customers are routinely denied other commonly requested forms of customer service such as conducting "price checks" and retrieving items from store shelves. In turn, a hostile conclusion routinely ends the interaction. In the case of Terri, her groceries were aggressively thrown into a shopping bag, resulting in damage to her canned goods. Terri's encounter is an example of how a consumer-oriented microinteractional assault can unfold.

The sequence of *greeting–dismissal–denial–hostility* represents the key microinteractional elements of these hostile encounters that make them identifiable. Yet it is important to note that, because of the fluid nature of interaction, one element does not always determine the other. Nonetheless, this sequence marks how consumer-based MIAs typically unfold for poor black women in the inner city, and this sort of interaction contrasts with middle-class expectations of "going to the store" which are grounded in friendly, polite, and attentive customer service. Violations of these expectations can be grounds for requesting to see the manager. Terri's account suggests that she is aware that this encounter violates the general expectations of civil public interaction. Though her routine experience with interactions unfolding in this way with local store personnel is still frustrating, she has become somewhat used to this type of encounter.

In the same way that residents adapt to the frequency of gun violence in the neighborhood, Terri has accommodated to the routine nature of these hostile encounters, which are best understood as a form of social injury, the microinteractional assault. MIAs work to communicate either explicitly or subtly, through verbal and nonverbal communication, a range of biased attitudes and beliefs held about marginalized groups. They are intended to attack the group identity of the targeted individual, be it race, gender, sexual orientation, or social class status through avoidant behavior, name calling, or other discriminatory actions. What I note as microinteractional assaults complements what Derald Wing Sue calls "microaggressions": the "brief, everyday exchanges that send denigrating messages to certain individuals because of their group membership (people of color, women, or LGBTs)" (2010, 24). Other scholars have described this phenomenon as put-downs (Pierce et al. 1978, 66), subtle insults (Solorzano, Ceja, and Yosso 2000), as well as microinequities (Hinton 2004). While previous studies focus primarily on the experiences of middle-class minorities with one "master status" (Hughes 1945) such as race, gender or sexuality, my analysis of MIAs extends previous discussion in the literature by focusing on a form of social injury that occurs at the intersection of race, gender, and class and reflects the complicated experience of having more than one marginalized status while living in a distressed inner-city neighborhood. My analysis is also distinct in its examination of the experiences of poor and working-class black women.

The microaggressions Sue (2010) describes tend to illustrate troubled verbal and nonverbal interactions involving at least one person with a marginalized identity; he does not, however, examine how intersecting categories influence interactions. Instead he considers each categorical identity separately, not taking into account the impact of belonging to more than one marginalized identity category. For example, within everyday public encounters a middle-class white woman can experience microaggressions targeting her gender and a middle-class black man may encounter race-oriented microaggressions; but a middle-class black woman endures microaggressions attacking both her marginalized race and gender identity.

Although these forms of microaggressions are significant independently, I argue that microaggressive encounters cannot be adequately conceptualized without acknowledging the intersections of multiple identities. I propose that social class status contributes heavily to how microaggressions unfold and influence who is targeted and the resulting consequences. Sue (2010) illustrates how microaggressions impact being on the margin through membership in a targeted identity category such as people of color or women, yet he describes these interactions in such a way that the normative targets happen to be members of the middle class and above. In this study I uncover how *poor black women* become routine targets of MIAs in an inner-city neighborhood. I also take into account how poverty intersects with place by showing how the consequences of MIAs are further complicated when experienced by persons who are poor, black, *and* live in a depressed urban setting. Through respondent accounts I show how intersections of race, gender, and class influence the structure and frequency of consumer-oriented MIAs and further complicate their impact. I illustrate not only how these assaults are interactional but also how the roles of participants within each interaction are not equal. The ways in which power operates in these interpersonal exchanges is central to illustrating how inequality is reproduced in day-to-day encounters in a key public setting: local businesses where consumer transactions are taking place.

FACE-TO-FACE INTERACTIONS

A microinteractional assault is a type of conscious and deliberate face-to-face interactional encounter, a social arrangement that consists of an exchange of words and glances between participants. Specifically, face engagements include "instances of two or more participants in a situation joining each other openly in maintaining a single focus of cognitive and visual attention" (Goffman 1963, 89). This exchange is understood to be a single mutual activity involving favored communication rights. Examples of typical face engagements include small talk, a waitress taking an order, a shop owner making a sale, or a formal discussion. An example of a troubled encounter would be a waiter walking away from a customer who is trying to place an order, one passerby bumping into another or pushing another down onto the sidewalk as they pass one another on the street, or a waitress spilling coffee on a patron and then laughing aloud.

MIAs take the form of what Erving Goffman calls "regular" occasions, a subcategory of social occasions. Regular occasions are "instances that form part of a series of like occasions, the series being seen as a unit and developing as such as a daily, weekly, or annual cycle" (Goffman 1963, 19). Such occurrences often include the same participants or participants exhibiting similar characteristics; other events, like impromptu parties or one-shot affairs, would not be considered regular occasions. Goffman highlights the varying participant roles on display during regular occasions, and notes that roles differ from one person to another within the same interaction. For example, when a school-age child enters an ice cream shop with the intention of making a purchase, her role may be one of leisure, while the middle-aged store employee standing behind the counter may be performing a role of work (Goffman 1963).

A central component of face-to-face interactions are that they are embodied. This means that they include the exchange of messages between persons present via bodily activity. Such messages can include laughter, spoken words, or a hard shove. These activities send meaningful messages to the other person(s) present in the exchange. In addition to physical activities as a form of exchange, physical presence can express belonging or outsider status. Finally, suitable management of personal appearance, or the neglect thereof, can convey compliance with dominant social norms for public presentation or poor self-control. Expression through what Goffman (1963) calls "unfocused interaction" can happen within a brief moment between passersby and without any spoken interchange.

Microinteractional assaults can occur during the regular activities required to manage daily life. Common settings where MIAs occur in inner-city neighborhoods include the local grocery store, the corner market, in and around neighborhood check-cashing establishments, and on the street. While conducting routine tasks in these settings, women experience a range of MIAs that vary in intensity and levels of intrusion. In this chapter, I describe two categories of microinteractional assaults, *hostile encounters* and *hypersurveillance*, as they occur in local businesses where consumer transactions take place. Women in this setting typically manage consumer-oriented MIAs through the strategy known as interactional resistance.

Hostile Encounters

Hostile encounters operate as a key form of microinteractional assaults; they are brief but routine forms of verbal and behavioral humiliation. Unlike degradation ceremonies, with MIAs women are subject to repeated shaming based on dominant ideas about who they are. Harold Garfinkel explains that a part of degradation ceremonies is to use moral indignation to denounce an individual before witnesses. In this way degradation ceremonies are about exposing a person for who the denouncer believes she really is, not who she appears to be (1956, 421–423). According to respondent accounts, women in East Oakland seem aware of how they are often perceived by employees in local businesses. Though most do not accept these ideas about themselves (e.g., as unworthy of civility, as inferior, etc.), they are familiar with and often expect the MIAs that often accompany outsider beliefs in their lesser status. With each individual MIA women experience it is not guaranteed that the next will be more degrading than the last. Nevertheless, in every new encounter with these assaults mainstream perceptions about poor black women are reinforced.

The cumulative effect of these encounters over one's lifetime work to intensify resulting feelings of humiliation, anger, frustration, and the like with each troubled interaction.

Hostile interactions can play out intentionally or unintentionally, but either way conveys contentious, negative, and insulting messages based on marginalized identity status (Sue 2010). Examples of hostile encounters at work are elevated voice, forceful and insulting language, or poor verbal and physical customer service (e.g., dropping groceries, grabbing money from a patron). Hostile encounters can be understood as a form of microinteractional assault that is often observed within consumer-oriented interactions. Sue (2010) asserts that when such behaviors become interpersonal encounters they reflect much more than the individual views and feelings of the perpetrator. When these hostilities unfold between persons within face-to-face encounters the harsh and derogatory messages being sent reflect a larger dichotomous worldview that includes dominant understandings of inferiority/superiority, normality/abnormality, and the like (Solorzano, Ceja, and Yosso 2000; Sue 2010).

Lionel D. Scott, in his study of racial identity and discrimination among African American adolescents (2003), notes that these types of microstressors that happen in public can be damaging to the psyche of African American adolescents as their effects intensify the adolescents' overall levels of stress (Scott 2003; see also Fee and Krieger 1994). The constant and cumulative nature of microaggressions results in severe, lifelong, systemic consequences for the targeted person or group (Nielsen 2004; Sue 2010). Unlike hate crimes or other overt forms of discrimination, hostile encounters are often seen as lesser offenses. Yet some resulting consequences can be the development of mental and physical health problems, anger, frustration, perpetuated stereotypes of marginalized groups, a hostile work climate, reduced productivity, and disengagement

(Sue 2010, chap. 3). The consequence of hostile encounters may be especially troublesome for poor, black women, since those who are most at risk for developing stress-related health conditions such as hypertension are women who have been found to internalize their responses to discrimination (versus those who actively speak out against unfair treatment; Fee and Krieger 1994, 17–18; Krieger 1990).

Dominant perceptions about poor, inner-city, black women that motivate instances of MIAs also work to reproduce a type of degraded femininity. Remaining visible on the street and when patronizing local businesses, women are exposed to demeaning mainstream perceptions about who they are in the form of MIAs. Through these interactions black women become redefined by these ideas, even if only for a moment. Repeated encounters where MIAs play out and target black women who often cannot escape when, where, and with whom these assaults occur begins to define particular conditions, behaviors, and expectations that come to reproduce a degraded normative understanding of black femininity. These troubled interactions have become a form of public social control within the confines of urban neighborhoods. Though these particular microassaults are not physically violent they do aim for a level of psychological control through repeated humiliation.

Due to a lack of resources women must enter local spaces where they are regularly targeted and made vulnerable to verbal and nonverbal assaults. Lack of reliable and consistent transportation often confines poor residents to their residential community; such limits placed on mobility force many women into stores and onto streets where they are regularly assaulted, stripping them of agency and control of their own movements. Such actions work to routinize oppression within what Patricia hill Collins describes as a culture of violence (2005, chap. 7). In this way, MIAs are much like the violence that forms the backdrop of neighborhood life.

The following excerpt from my field notes illustrates a hostile encounter as it unfolded in a local grocery store that involved a black woman in her early twenties negotiating a purchase with her Electronic Benefit Transfer (EBT) card at a local grocery store in her East Oakland neighborhood:

> I wait in the checkout line of the neighborhood grocery store and look on as a black woman in her early 20s calmly tells the middle-aged white female store clerk who is ringing up her items that she wants to buy some milk along with her other groceries lying on the conveyor belt. The young woman explains to the checker that the gallon-size 2% milk that she wants has an expiration date of tomorrow printed on the outside of the container. The checker proceeds to tell the young woman that if she doesn't want to get that particular container of milk then she should get another one with an expiration date that she prefers. The customer then asks the store clerk if she can have someone go in the back to see if there are any more gallons of 2% milk with a later expiration date, because all of the containers she sees on the shelf have the same date as the one in front of her, and she really needs to buy the milk today. The checker replies to the woman in a voice loud enough for me to hear while waiting in line several steps away, "No. You have to get what is on the shelf or come back another day." The customer replies in a calm voice, "I just don't want to waste my money on a gallon of milk that is going to spoil in one or two days." The checker replies, "You're not paying with your money, you're paying with *that*," and she points to the EBT card the woman is holding.

Multiple markers of verbal hostility are displayed in this scene. The elevated and antagonistic tone of voice of the store employee directs at the customer is belligerent in nature.

Additionally, the store clerk refuses to check on a product requested by the customer and instead informs the customer that her only option is to retrieve another of the same food product (which the customer has already deemed unsatisfactory) from the store shelf. This behavior directly opposes norms of civility, particularly in the context of customer service. Such conduct raises the question of why a departure from civil customer service practices is taking place. The roles in this interpersonal exchange are unequal: the customer is being treated as if she is a member of an inferior group (i.e., like a child), and the store employee seems to view the customer as unworthy of civility based on the verbal and nonverbal exchanges they are having. The store employee's assertion of power in this interaction in the form of refusing a customer request further reinforces the lesser status of the young woman trying to buy a gallon of milk.

Historically, the identity markers of this customer—some of which include black, female, and poor—have been markers of inferiority and lesser power. The assumed phenotypical identity category of whiteness held by the store clerk has historically defined cultural normativity and power yielding (Sue 2010). These varying cultural positions are at work here as the store clerk assumes a position of authority while she dictates what she will and will not do and gives unsolicited directions to the customer within this interaction.

Throughout this interaction each person in the exchange has normative ideas about the other as well as about herself. This includes attitudes, behavior, and types of self-presentation that align with who each understands the other (and self) to be (e.g., woman, man, black, white, poor, nonpoor, store employee, customer, etc.). In the case of the store checker, as she asserts a sense of power over the customer by refusing to perform civil customer service practices she makes an evaluation about who she is in this interaction (a person of authority, superior) and who the customer is (of lesser status, inferior). As this exchange continues to unfold the customer remains calm, which seems to send a message of compliance to the store clerk further reaffirming her feelings of superiority. This superiority is expressed further as she reminds the customer that she is making a purchase using government assistance (the EBT card) and not money.

EBT is a form of public assistance that can be used to pay for food. The store employee implies that the act of using EBT gives the young woman a status as "less than" a typical customer. This statement suggests that her status as an EBT cardholder makes her unworthy of the privileges "regular" customers are afforded. Such privileges include making requests of store employees and other forms of civility that most customers may assume and generally receive when patronizing a business. This interaction illustrates more than just a troubled exchange between customer and store employee; it represents what the roles of white female store clerk and poor black female customer look like in this space through interaction. As the meanings of poor black customer and white female store clerk are produced in this interaction, their respective statuses as superior and inferior are reproduced. This reflects what Candace West and Don Zimmerman (1987) describe in their discussion of gender and the division of labor. They explain that when individuals engage in activities, more than just the action is taking place; specific roles are being produced and reproduced, including who is dominant and who is subordinate. With each microinteractional assault that occurs there is more than just a troubled interaction taking place in a grocery store. The role of poor black women who live in this distressed setting and who frequent this business is reinforced as subordinate while the role of store employees is reinforced as dominant (West and Zimmerman 2002). For example, as a result of much of the social stigma around government aid programs, making public the customer's status as an EBT card user may have been one of the more demeaning things the store clerk could do. In turn, this action reinforces her own position of power in this space over this particular type of customer.

Michelle, a nineteen-year-old mother of a newborn, also uses EBT to pay for food at this local grocery store, and she recounted for me a hostile encounter she experienced while trying to make a purchase:

> When it was my turn in line, the checker began to ring up my groceries as I watched the screen that displays the price of each item. I then realized that I had picked up the wrong package of diapers, so I asked the checker to please take this package off of the bill and if he could call somebody to go get the correct one that I need. He then starts breathing hard and rolling his eyes. He calls over the loudspeaker for someone to bring the diapers I asked for up to the register. No one comes. A minute or so later he calls again, but still no response. I then decide to go get it myself. When I return just moments later, all of the groceries he had already scanned had been removed from the register. When I asked him where all my groceries were, he said he didn't know what I was talking about but if I wanted to buy something I needed to go wait in line like everybody else.

The interaction Michelle describes is another example of how hostile encounters can unfold in this space. As is common in these encounters, the store clerk has more power in this context, which is not likely to be so in the broader society. As a way to reaffirm his precarious hold on power he asserts his dominance within interactions with women in this particular setting.[1]

Michelle explained to me that she was momentarily "frozen" when the store clerk said he didn't know where her groceries were and sent her to the end of the line. "At first I wanted to believe this was a joke, until I snapped back to reality and remembered that this is how things work here," she recounted. She explained to me that she was really angry as she looked at the long line she would have to go back and wait in, and she thought about the time wasted gathering her groceries initially, only to have to do it all over again. At this point Michelle decided to leave the store without the goods she came for. "I didn't have the energy to fight with him or wait in line again. I went back another day when I had the energy to deal with this kind of thing." Michelle's description of this interaction reflects the routine nature of hostile encounters in this space. The scene also indicates how accommodation to circumstances and place are shaped for local residents. Making the decision to leave the store only to return another day when prepared to "deal with this kind of thing" demonstrates her familiarity with this type of interaction.

The consumer-oriented encounter Michelle describes is another example of the frustration and trauma that can accompany daily tasks such as grocery shopping for many women in the inner city. When I asked women in East Oakland how they feel when they are put down, dismissed, or denied service by store employees in the neighborhood many replied just as twenty-four-year-old Jennifer did: "Yeah, I don't like it and I sure as hell don't deserve to be treated bad and talked to crazy when I am just asking nicely about something I am paying for, but where else am I going to go?" This question is one that was posed to me repeatedly when I asked about the troubled interactions women experienced in local stores. A significant element of these kinds of interactions is that no matter how customers like Michelle and Jennifer may feel about being dismissed or humiliated during encounters, the community conditions considerably limit residents from being able to shop anywhere else. Poor families tend to suffer this type of limited mobility and restricted access in many socially isolated low-income communities.

Hypersurveillance

Hypersurveillance—keeping extreme watch over others, predominantly under the guise of suspicion—is another type of microinteractional assault that is practiced in the inner city and experienced by women. Throughout the interviews conducted for this study, respondents overwhelmingly reported feelings of anger and frustration with their treatment in local stores in two ways: first, when spending their money (as a paying customer), and second, as potential customers browsing in a store. Several participants noted being closely followed and asked if they needed help by store employees many more times than what they felt was to be generally expected. Two women described being startled by store employees who seemed to "appear from nowhere" while they were shopping. As a twenty-one-year-old respondent described her everyday experience of intense surveillance when she enters neighborhood stores, "Every day, people always look at me crazy and follow me around in stores. They ask me way too many times if I need help." She went on to illustrate the routine nature in which she is surveilled as she goes about her daily business. With obvious irritation she told of the "crazy" looks she receives and repeated questioning about her need for assistance while inside the establishment. Her claim that this sort of experience happens "every day" represents how MIAs in the form of hypersurveillance have become routine. Although such encounters are visibly upsetting to respondents, as in this case, they have become expected interactions in the urban environment.

In addition to cases of hypersurveillance becoming standard for black women within and beyond the boundaries of the neighborhood there is another level of interaction that accompanies the visual and verbal scrutiny that takes place: the role of physical intervention as a component of surveillance. One nineteen-year-old woman described to me how she feels about a store employee carrying her merchandise to the register for her and about being followed while in the store. "When I go downtown to [large retail chain] shoe store, me and my friends always get followed around and watched extra close," she explained. "A couple of times the people at the store carried my stuff to the register for me, but I didn't see them doing that for anyone else. They probably thought that I was going to try and steal it, but I wasn't. I don't get down like that; I have a job." This respondent stated her awareness that she is likely perceived by store employees to be a thief because she is a young black woman. She challenged this assessment by stressing that she is employed and doesn't steal, as stealing is something she feels is presumed in such an encounter.

Elijah Anderson argues that in public places black men are often assumed to be poor or criminal simply because they are black.[2] Since these evaluations are often made in very brief public interactions, there is rarely time to disprove these assumptions (Anderson 2011, 255). I propose that this is also true for black women in public places. For example, the young woman in the shoe store expressed her familiarity with such assessments as she recounted her story of being closely monitored by store personnel while shopping. When talking with her about this encounter I observed how she aimed to invalidate the reasons why she was surveilled while in the store. She explained to me that she was employed and had been for years, and she was proud that she did not take part in criminal activity and had no intention of doing so. Like the young men Anderson writes about, she too is seen as someone who carries the stigma of what Anderson describes as the "iconic ghetto" (2011, 255). As a black woman, her race and class status is associated with criminality, poverty, violent behavior, and the like. When the woman entered the shoe store it was quite likely that her presence was met with apprehension and suspicion because store employees associated her with the iconic ghetto and thought she was prone to criminal behavior and as a result warranted careful monitoring.

In this case the woman recounted more than just being "watched" while in the store; she described a type of hyper-surveillance. Yet this scrutiny is poorly camouflaged as careful and exaggeratedly attentive customer service. Such methods of surveillance are strategic. This manipulation of traditional and civil customer service is careful not to abandon common rituals associated with civility in this setting, like offering help to a customer upon her entrance to the store; this way the customer cannot accuse store employees of being rude, unhelpful, or inattentive. Nevertheless, the woman did not feel as if she received good customer service simply because so much attention was likely paid to her out of suspicion. As a result, she felt as if civility had been abandoned entirely. Though the aim of store personnel may have been for their actions to go undetected as surveillance and instead seen as attentive, the consumer described feeling singled out by the attention she received (Feagin and Sikes 1994, 45–49; Sue 2010, 79). Whether deliberately poor or camouflaged customer service takes place, the targeted patron often leaves feeling hypervisible.

The customer in this case acknowledged that the very specific service she received was not universal; nor was it unsuspecting. Although technically she was being served in a responsive manner, she knew that she was still being surveilled and appraised because of who she is. She saw this as unjust. Yet in this downtown retail store the evaluation being made about this woman and her friends is often the same evaluation made when they enter stores in their residential neighborhood. The appraisal is that these women are criminal and should be closely monitored while inside any retail business. In essence, these women are carrying around the iconic ghetto with them wherever they go. The perception that they represent a form of poverty and crime is a type of social baggage that they never leave home without.

In their work on racism and the black middle class, Joe R. Feagin and Melvin P. Sikes point out that a central problem that black people encounter while shopping is the widespread assumption by whites that their intent is to steal. With this assumption must come uncomfortable consequences. Beyond the reality of surveillance while still in the store, there is a constant reminder that you are black and unequal in a nonblack world. Further, the recurring feelings of frustration, anger, humiliation, and powerlessness stay with you long after leaving the specific racist encounter (Feagin and Sikes 1994, 72–77).

Such testimonies exhibit some of the implications that come with being marked as suspicious or threatening, to the point of being under careful watch while in public. As these respondents carry out the daily tasks of shopping, store employees and possibly others treat them with skepticism. The respondents note this type of treatment when shopping in both the neighborhoods in which they live and in other communities. This brings up the question of where one belongs. Being treated as a problem, inconvenience, or threat is an assault on oneself and one's character. While simultaneously being a consumer, this sends a powerful message that, based on visible identity markers, one person's patronage is not as valuable as that of another. Gardener talks about communication in public being very "appearance dependent" based on physical qualities, nonverbal indicators, and overall appearance; she points out that this encourages judgment from both parties and makes stereotypes predictable (1995, 52–53).

In situated encounters like this one a woman's race, class, and gender are communicated and defined before she enters a store. Her presence in the store operates as a type of trigger that elicits a reaction from the store employees based on predetermined associations between what they perceive to be the woman's race, class, and gender and wider ideas such as crime, violence, and poverty. As both verbal and nonverbal interactions unfold between consumer and store employees, the consumer becomes accountable to the normative ideas that store personnel have about young, black, women. Her presence in this space gives those she encounters there an opportunity to make the predetermined associations they have about her real. This woman and others like her experience daily encounters where they walk into expectations informed by gender, race, and class and shaped by controlling images. Interactions like this one contribute to the reproduction of inequality. These public scenes operate as a mechanism through which dominant oppressive beliefs produce individual consequences from day to day (West and Fenstermaker 1995). The repetitive nature of these sorts of episodes for members of disadvantaged groups reinforces their subordinate social status to self and others alike.

Often it is assumed that only black men are exposed to these types of encounters. I suggest that women are also exposed to this sort of surveillance simply by virtue of their subordinate position in a race/class hierarchy. The stereotype of "black dangerousness" can produce an image of a hostile, violent, and angry black man (Sue 2010, 259), but the widespread understanding of blackness in general being associated with crime and violent behavior does not exclude women. Black women's oppression can take the form of racism in one instance, sexism in another, or gendered racism (Feagin and McKinney 2003, 19). The strength of oppressive race, class, and gender forces at work in the lives of women of color is what Denise A. Segura describes as "triple oppression"; she notes that the cumulative impact of this particular form of oppression places women of color in a "subordinate social and economic position relative to men of color and the white population" (1986, 48). Though black men may be the go-to image representing the "black dangerousness" stereotype, black women are very much associated with the ideas of violence and criminal behavior linked to this perception. The expectation of black women as criminal and violent is informed by prevailing controlling images. The cumulative impact of this association works to further complicate black women's oppression.

INTERACTIONAL RESISTANCE IN CONSUMER-ORIENTED MICROINTERACTIONAL ASSAULTS

Black women are regularly exposed to microinteractional assaults, and they develop a set of strategies to protect themselves from injury or harm. These strategies of defense include physical and, more commonly, verbal confrontations in response to MIAs. I use the term *interactional resistance* to refer to these verbal and physical oppositions to MIAs. Women from the inner city use interactional resistance to challenge being overcharged in the grocery store and as a way to call attention to being treated with less than common courtesy by employees while shopping.

Considering the routine experiences black women have with microinteractional assaults in local businesses, their value as consumers seems insignificant. According to the McKinsey Global Institute's (2009) analysis of consumer spending and U.S. economic growth from 2000 to 2007, consumer spending accounted for a contribution of over 75 percent. With a U.S. economy so reliant on consumer spending one would think that the role of any consumer is an important one. The everyday MIAs that women encounter while shopping in the inner city is a reminder that the value of consumer status is often associated with race, gender, and, class identity. The routine troubled encounters women experience with store personnel while shopping in urban communities indicate that they are often perceived as unworthy of the common courtesy most customers receive. This unworthiness goes beyond the level of face-to-face interaction. Based on their race, class, and gender, black women also seem to be appraised as less valuable consumers. In sum, women in the inner city describe encounters with harassment and, in general, being treated as insignificant. Being perceived as a consumer who is not valued increases the negative impact of MIAs.

Interactional resistance plays out in distinct ways for black women shopping in poor urban neighborhoods. The following excerpt from my field notes documents a hostile encounter in which Mecca, a black woman and neighborhood resident, acknowledges and contests being overcharged for a store item. This excerpt displays how the store clerk refuses to correct or even give further attention to the possibility of overcharging Mecca, even after she brings it to his attention. This dismissal of Mecca's request by the store clerk suggests that he believes his actions to be acceptable. His construction of her as someone worthy of being dismissed suggests she is being evaluated within the context of a controlling image (Collins 2004, 123), an image that was conceived before this interaction and will likely remain once it is over:

> I wait in the checkout line at the neighborhood grocery store close enough to hear the interaction unfold at the head of the line. The woman at the head of the line getting her items rung up lives in the neighborhood and I know her as Mecca. I hear her say to the store clerk helping her, "No, that is $15.99, not $21.99. I saw it in the sale paper the other day and the sticker on the shelf says $15.99—go look for yourself." Agitated, the checker replies to the young woman, "It doesn't matter what the sticker says or what the paper says. I have to charge you what is listed in my computer." Mecca answers back, "I don't care what your computer says, and y'all shouldn't put in the paper prices that aren't true." The checker then says, "I don't know what you

saw, but I still have to charge you the $21.99." Mecca retorts, "Yeah, whatever. But I'm gonna bring the paper in here so you can give me back the difference." The checker says, "You have to take that up with the manager." As the checker puts Mecca's bottle of tequila (the item for which the price is under debate) in a grocery bag she says to him, "Why can you overcharge me but I have to go to the manager to get it right? And, knowing him, that will probably never happen. This whole thing is fucked up." The checker looks at Mecca with a smirk on his face as she leaves the store. The man waiting in front of me steps up in the line to have his merchandise rung up. The store clerk looks at the middle-aged black man and says aloud, "Some people." The man replied, "She was right. I saw the same price she said was advertised in the sale paper." The checker mumbles, "Whatever. Not my problem." The man shakes his head and remains silent.

This excerpt depicts an encounter in which Mecca employs interactional resistance. She asserts herself to the store employee whom she believes is charging her more than the quoted sale price. The store clerk does not offer to do a price check or to consult a manager or another employee in an effort to clear up this matter. He and Mecca engage in back-and-forth talk regarding this price, yet the store employee does not change his position. Further, he makes it clear to Mecca and to others who can hear him that this is not his problem; it is hers. If she wants someone to look into the matter she must return to the store at another time and consult with the store manager.

The ways in which the store clerk engages in a particular set of "rules" regarding a price dispute with Mecca operates as a form of social control over poor black customers. He asserts his dominant status as the intermediary between Mecca and the product she wants to purchase. In situations like this one he makes the final determination as to what price will be charged for the item in question. For many local residents who have limited access to other grocery stores they are forced to abide by the "rules" at work even if they are manipulated based on the race, class, and gender of the customer.

The issue of invoking the store manager is significant here. Taking into account when and why the store clerk suggests that Mecca consult the manager is complicated, because not every customer with a discrepancy is referred to a store manager; this only happens in particular cases. Here I consider some of Mecca's categorical identities to be culprits in why she must seek out a manager to obtain a fair resolution. Why can't this relatively simple matter be solved with the store employee before her? This brings up the different outcomes in regard to fairness for different people based on categorical identity. When Mecca verbally disputes the price being charged, she interrupts the normal flow of an interaction, momentarily upsetting the raced and gendered power structure within the interaction. When the white male clerk's declaration of the price to be charged is not readily accepted by this traditionally subordinate black woman, he then calls on a structural resource of power in this setting: the store manager.

Ultimately, Mecca does purchase the item, yet she makes clear through her verbal interaction with the store clerk that there is a problem. She does this in a voice loud enough for all those in a reasonable distance to hear that she is aware that she is being wronged. Even after Mecca exits the store her position becomes reinforced without her knowledge. The middle-aged black man who waits patiently behind Mecca in the grocery line displays solidarity with her when he tells the store clerk that the price he charged her is incorrect and that the young woman was valid in her request. Even though Mecca leaves the store after purchasing the item under dispute, her interaction reveals that she does not ignore what is happening.

Mecca does not back down from being overcharged by the white male store clerk, who appears to be in is early forties. In this case she still purchases the product, which is not an uncommon practice even when being overcharged. As a result of limited resources caused by the social isolation that often accompanies racialized poverty in East Oakland, there are few other stores in which to shop. By purchasing this product that she believes she is being overcharged for, Mecca can appear to the store clerk and others not close enough to hear the interaction as being loud and aggressive for no "real" reason. Such interactions can be perceived in a way that reinforces controlling images of black working class women as "bitches." Though Mecca is asserting herself by pointing out a price discrepancy because of her particular race, class, and gender, as many consumers would, she can easily be perceived as "confrontational and actively aggressive" in interactions like this (Collins 2004, 123). Her encounter in the grocery store is an instance of everyday racism informed by her class and gender. Mecca's method of confronting this situation was direct and unwavering. Feagin and Sikes suggest that this is one of many strategies often employed by blacks in the face of daily discrimination from whites. In their study of racism and the black middle class, Feagin and Sikes (1994) describe how when encountering routine racist slights in public, some believe it is important to demand respect and educate the other party on his ignorant behavior (1994, 47–49). They note that over time this method causes a slightly lesser degree of psychological stress and harm than some more suppressive methods.

There are a number of businesses that my respondents in East Oakland regularly frequented. Many women complained of consistently poor service by store employees when shopping in the local grocery store. When I inquired about what this "poor service" looked like, Myisha, a twenty-four-year-old

woman who has lived in East Oakland her entire life, explained
what shopping is often like for her:

> When I go to the store and I need something that they
> don't have out on the shelf I just leave. I don't ask anyone to
> check and see if they have it anymore, because it's always a
> problem. Either they just say they don't have it without
> checking or they say they are going to go look and then
> they never come back to let me know either way. Same
> goes if something is up on a high shelf and I can't reach it;
> I look around for a ladder or stool to give me a lift so I can
> get the item myself. I do this because if I ask someone who
> works at the store to get it for me, they say to give them a
> few minutes to get a ladder but never usually return to help
> me. It is so frustrating because I am spending my money
> just like everybody else, but it's like they don't even care.

Myisha explains that she often feels dismissed while interacting with the store's personnel as she attempts to buy goods
there. This experience of dismissal is a key feature of consumer-
oriented MIAs and in part shapes how these encounters unfold.
Myisha employs a form of interactional resistance by limiting
verbal interaction with store employees; she draws on her past
experiences of having her questions and requests dismissed,
and at times ignored or denied, to inform her current resistant
actions. Here she explains her resistant reactions in two ways.
First, if she doesn't see what she came to the store to purchase
out on the shelf she leaves the store, no questions asked. If she
can't find the items she's looking for she does not consult with
store employees; in fact, she tries to keep encounters with them
to a minimum. If she sees goods she wants but they are located
out of her reach, she takes on the responsibility of finding a
way to access the items herself by locating a stool or ladder. In
doing this she blurs the boundaries of traditional customer
behavior and the behavior of store staff: at this moment she is

required to perform the tasks she is essentially paying for as a store patron.

Both Mecca and Myisha must live with the consequences of the different ways in which they manage consumer-oriented MIAs. These small acts of resistance appear unsuccessful in disrupting fundamental inequalities. Rather, they risk reinforcing stereotypes about black women as angry, loud, confrontational, and so on. When women in the neighborhood have encounters in local stores where they believe they are being overcharged or generally mistreated by store employees, they become angry. Some react aggressively, reinforcing widespread beliefs about who they are.

The two forms of interactional resistance that Myisha performs—leaving the store when she can't find what she needs or climbing up on a store ladder to reach items that store employees won't get for her—are complicated and interconnected. These actions, which are a result of situational circumstances, contrast with expectations of hegemonic femininity. Myisha does not defer to store employees when she cannot find an item she needs or if a product is out of her reach. Instead she enters the store with no intention of seeking help even if she needs it; she steps outside the boundaries of typical customer behavior by climbing atop store ladders to reach available products. Such actions do not project the submissive demeanor commonly linked to white middle-class femininity. Myisha's actions illustrate not only that such characteristics of normative femininity may not be desirable but also that they are not possible if she is to successfully acquire the goods she needs from local stores where she is evaluated as an inferior consumer and unworthy of civility (Collins 2004, 193–197). Myisha indicates that on the occasions that she leaves the store empty-handed she must still return; this continued patronage after multiple instances of poor service suggests that she has few, if any, local options for places in which to purchase her groceries. She acknowledges with precision her experiences of frequent troubled encounters in stores, yet still she must endure them repeatedly. This is why daily life can often feel like a grind for poor black women.

The types of interactional resistance that Myisha performs also operate as strategies she uses to manage recurring consumer-oriented MIAs. Her strategies provide her with ways to keep such assaults at bay, at least some of the time, while still being able to access groceries and other goods needed to survive from day to day. The forms of interactional resistance Myisha carries out are complicated by her not having the luxury of boycotting this business in the traditional sense. Instead she rejects interaction with immediate representatives of the establishment—its employees. Additionally, while resisting the interactional power present she remains proactive in getting her needs met. She does this by declaring her own sense of dominance in this space by using store-owned ladders and stools to reach what she needs herself. She creatively exerts what power she has in an effort to keep her interactions with store employees minimal while still trying to get the goods she desires. When I talked with Myisha about how she felt about the kinds of interactions she had with store personnel, she explained, "It doesn't feel good being ignored, and all you're trying to do is buy food and you're not bothering anybody." She went on to say that even though she doesn't like it, this is the reality if she is going to continue living in this community. So, for now, she tries to avoid any verbal exchange with store employees as best she can.

Myisha is not alone in her experiences of feeling dismissed and ignored while shopping. "Black shoppers at all income levels report being ignored when in need of service," note Feagin and Sikes (1994, 48). Yet such feelings do not simply fade away at the close of an interaction. Associated emotions like pain, frustration, anger, and humiliation can be long lasting. Single incidents of hostility and discrimination can often produce lifelong memories that inform the lives and perspectives of those targeted. The Rotter Introversion–Extroversion Scale, which measures whether people feel in control of their lives, has found that blacks and whites score differently. Research studies using this scale describe how blacks primarily seem to feel that their lives are controlled by outside forces. A key component here is that when one feels little to no control over his life there is a struggle in maintaining a sense of personal well-being and achieving desired life goals. Continued fighting against daily MIAs rooted in discrimination can result in a very real sense of powerlessness (Feagin and Sikes 1994, 76). The experiences of present-day MIAs are also directly linked to historical trauma, including the generational inheritance of histories of discrimination. As a result, for every assault that occurs today, every past wound—even those of prior generations—is deepened. Finally, it must be taken into account that experiences of microaggressive stress that happen to marginalized groups compound ordinary stressful life events that occur for almost everyone, and together they result in a profound if not inhuman amount of stress for any person to endure (Sue 2010, 96). In the case, specifically, of poor black women, situational circumstances encourage them to violate gender expectations, which makes them more vulnerable to sanctions. For example, poor black women who have worked outside the home for generations and as a result are not financially subordinated within black families and communities have been marked as less feminine because they have to work. Such work outside the home violates assumptions of hegemonic femininity. This kind of work makes it hard to view black women as delicate or attractive. Hegemonic black femininity marks the least desirable form of femininity as it is composed of prevailing images of black women as bitches, whores, bad mothers, and the like (Collins 2005, 193–199). This status of being on the bottom of the social hierarchy places black women at risk to the violence and oppression reserved for those who are not "real women."

Intersections of race, class, and gender inform even the most simple and routine life tasks. For black women living in urban communities, significant time out of their daily lives is spent experiencing and refuting microinteractional assaults as they maneuver through public space. As women carry out the routine public tasks associated with managing their daily lives they experience different types of MIAs. Understanding the key features of these encounters, how they typically unfold, and the consequences of such interactions reveals in part what inner-city life is like for poor black women. Through these encounters we see how race, class, and gender directly influence and complicate how women experience some of the daily demands of inner-city life, including how they have become familiar with the trauma of these assaults not only within the encounters themselves but also through their lasting consequences.

To be routinely targeted by verbal and behavioral humiliation works as a way of evaluating who these women are and who they are not. With each troubled public interaction where race, class, and gender are communicated, defined, and evaluated, we simultaneously see the courtesies of public civility disregarded. Such encounters reproduce inequality via the reinforcement of dominant perceptions of women in the urban space. With every MIA that occurs, a larger message is conveyed that poor black women are unworthy of civil public interaction. To be marked as unworthy of a form of basic human courtesy is both a powerful and extremely harmful label. Such a status increases the vulnerability of black women to harassment and abuse in the public space.

As a result of countless encounters over their lives, women in my study were aware that MIAs are likely to await them when entering a local grocery or corner store. This repeated experience and its harmful consequences can become overwhelming. For women already struggling to manage daily lives complicated by poverty, underemployment, and violence, routinely encountering hostility, dismissal, and denial when trying to purchase necessities intensifies the constant daily stress they already live with. Scholars have found that the constant and cumulative nature of these kinds of encounters causes intense levels of stress for members of marginalized groups. Such stress over time has been proven to negatively impact one's physical, emotional, and psychological health (Sue 2010, 105–109). Yet in large part these effects have been found when evaluating members of the middle-class and above. For poor black women who already live under harsh conditions in underserved communities, routine experiences with MIAs intensify their already difficult lives. Consequently, these customary encounters seem to be extremely detrimental to their overall health. Daily experiences with MIAs over the course of a lifetime appear to be a very harmful and life-altering punishment for being poor, female, and black in an urban setting.

CHAPTER 3

"I Am Not a Prostitute"

HOW YOUNG BLACK WOMEN CHALLENGE SEXUAL HARASSMENT ON THE STREET

AT APPROXIMATELY EIGHT thirty on a weekday morning a black man who appears to be in his late thirties approaches me as I sit at the rear of a city bus. His skin is a light brown complexion and he wears his dark curly hair in a short style. He is dressed in khakis, a white button-down shirt, and a wool coat, and he is carrying a black computer bag. He takes a seat right behind me in the very last row of the coach. Gripping the metal safety bar on the top of my seat with both hands he leans over my left shoulder and asks in a low voice, "How much are you charging for an hour?" In a mix of anger and frustration I quickly jolt my head around to face him and reply, "That's not my business." Not convinced, he goes on to inform me that he would "make it worth my while." In a loud voice I reply, "I am not a prostitute." He then scolds me for raising my voice: "You don't have to get loud with me," he says as he removes his sunglasses and looks me over once more while shaking his head.

At the time of this interaction I am riding the city bus along a central thoroughfare in West Oakland, an area that has long struggled with drug activity, poverty, and violence. The street is lined on one side with large industrial buildings and on the other with single-family homes and a few small apartment buildings. I observe from the bus window a small park where men and women are asleep on benches and some are curled up on patches of brown grass; others stand talking and drinking from containers covered by paper bags. I see a few women standing along the sidewalk. Each of these women appears to be black, and they range in age from their late twenties to at least their mid-thirties. Two of the women stand together; others stand alone, with at least a block or so between them. Though this area is not the city's central site for prostitution, it appears to attract what look to be a few sex workers in addition to those who look to be longtime drug abusers. These observations inform the interaction I have with the man on the bus. My experiences in the field indicate to me that I have been propositioned for sex. The man on the bus perceives me to be a sex worker, in part by evaluating my race, gender, and presence in this particular place; his perceptions and expectations are informed by what he understands each of those categories and the corresponding identity markers I display to him mean. After I tell him that I am not in the business of prostitution his idea about who and what I am keeps him from being so sure. This interaction was one of my earliest experiences in the field. Looking back, I realize I encountered a distinct type of microinteractional assault (MIA). I now see this encounter as a case of street-based MIAs that are part of the daily lives of many black women living in urban communities.

For numerous inner-city residents time spent walking along local streets is customary. A part of this routine action is the presence of street-based encounters and interactions with others. For many black women this means regular experiences with street-based MIAs. These assaults encompass what Deborah Tuerkheimer (1997) defines as street harassment: when a woman in public is intruded upon by a man's words, noises, or gestures. Yet where others may use *sexual harassment* as an all-encompassing term to describe hostile gender-specific

encounters on the street, I unpack the meaning of these encounters for women in this setting and (re)conceptualize these
encounters as microinteractional assaults. The use of the term
assault in the description of these encounters highlights the
shared context of violence for residents and how the experience with violence is shaped by gender. Men living in the
inner city may be more vulnerable to gun violence while women
are more vulnerable to gender-specific assaults in public space.
Street-based MIAs include a range of negative interactional
exchanges that reflect power differentials between black women
and the men they encounter on the street. Unlike most consumer-
based MIAs, many of these interactions are shaped by the act
or threat of sexual violence. This includes sexualized comments and behavior made by boys and men who range in age
from their teens to middle age. How do women make sense of
the troubled encounters they have with men on the street? What
strategies do women employ in an effort to manage routine
threats of physical and sexual violence?

Dominant images of black women as hypersexual others
play out in their experiences with street-based MIAs. Indeed,
these "controlling images" (Collins 2005) of black women shape
expectations and evaluations of who these women are and are
not. With each encounter these women are reminded of their
unequal status. Controlling images reinforce black women's
status as available to men, making them vulnerable to inappropriate and harmful social behavior. As oppressive images are
continuously reproduced they shape black women's encounters
with others, including street-based public interactions. Through
these interactions the marginalization of black women continues to operate on the interpersonal level.

In this chapter, I also examine the particular strategies that
women use to manage street-based MIAs. The defensive strategies at work differ when performed beyond consumer-based

MIAs and outside the boundaries of local businesses. I concentrate on how these tactics operate within street-based encounters beyond the margins of civility that often come with consumer-based interactions. I first examine the strategic work I refer to as interactional resistance: how women speak and act out in response to experiences of public assault. The second strategy is what I call buffering. This tactic is a form of interactional resistance and operates as a type of physical and psychological shielding, as protection from the hurt and degradation that accompanies street-based MIAs. In addition, buffering helps individuals recover from experiences with troubled encounters.

Understanding Sexual Violence

Within the U.S. social order there is a history of raced and gendered subordination. This oppression influences contemporary social interactions as well as evaluations of marginalized persons. A current example of one way this subordination has an impact on black womanhood is through the experiences of living within a culture of rape. Patricia Hill Collins (2005) contends that rape is much more than a single act; rather, it comprises a multitude of sexual assaults on black womanhood. This includes sexual harassment, both verbal and physical; sexual extortion; stranger, intimate partner, and acquaintance rape; and widely held misogynistic beliefs about women. Through consciously or unconsciously adopting this rape culture framework, the conditions under which women are objectified and abused become reinforced. The key component of this culture and its extremely harmful consequences is female domination. Largely, American beliefs about masculinity rely upon male dominance over women sexually, physically, and institutionally. For black women and men who already experience mainstream racial oppression, this type of gender ideology allows for intraracial gender domination targeting black women. This is done in an effort to develop and maintain a masculine identity for black men, whose maleness is consistently challenged within a racist social structure. In this context, domination of black women by black men seems like a logical step in the American social order of operations. In part, this step mirrors the dominant image of male power over women.

Black women become extremely vulnerable within a gender ideology where black men are fighting for a routinely oppressed mainstream masculine status. For black men to capture and maintain this status while managing life in a disadvantaged inner-city community, women can become targets of sexually predatory male behavior. This behavior can come at the hands of young men as they struggle to develop a masculine identity or older men who struggle to prove, and in some cases rebuild, their masculine identity (Collins 2005; Sheffield 1987, 177).

The routine mass media portrayals of black women employing a variety of controlling images work to reinforce the widespread internalization of them as subordinate and worthy of oppression and assault. This increases their vulnerability to street-based MIAs at the hands of black men in their neighborhoods. The added complication of lower-class status and the daily lived oppressions that come with it intensify the urgency of many men to claim their masculine status, even to the detriment of black women. Understanding assaults on black womanhood through the context of a rape culture underscores the severity of sexual dominance against black women (Collins 2005, 228–232). This concept reveals the long-standing systemic nature of sexual violence against black women. In addition, it tells of the far-reaching critical consequences of the history of institutionalized rape and oppression of black men.

When considering the ways in which female domination is a central component in maintaining the larger culture of rape, we are reminded of the pivotal role of violence—both actual and threatened. Carole J. Sheffield (1987) denotes "sexual terrorism" as a system of fear—specifically, fear of personal injury. When women experience fear they become dominated by the fear-inducing entity reinforcing their social control. Black women must endure the potentially violent trauma of both racism and sexual violence; both forms of oppression are a part of the same structure designed to keep them subordinate. In the context of rape, historically a black woman could not be raped, assaulted, or sexually exploited in any way by any man under U.S. law. This status of being "unrapable" marked black women and girls as essentially inferior (Sheffield 1987, 171–180).

Through the accounts of daily experiences with these troubled encounters, women in East Oakland have described potentially violent encounters as well as how they see themselves as vulnerable to sexual assault. Jocelyn A. Hollander explains that this vulnerability to violence is a central element of femininity; women's vulnerability is constructed through routine interactions where dominant ideas about gender are communicated, performed, and thus reinforced (2001, 84). For women in East Oakland, vulnerability is shaped via day-to-day interactions that often unfold on the street. These interactions are a reminder of the significant relationship between the body and violence, including threats of violence and the routine accomplishment of gender. A key component in the vulnerability of young women in the context of sexual violence is that they are often seen to be at a peak of sexual desirability. This perception of heightened risk is a result of the intersection of their gender, age, and sexuality (Hollander 2001, 84–95).

The victimization experienced by young women and the particular kinds of strategies they use to manage violence or attempt to avoid it are specifically shaped by their status as both young and women (Chesney-Lind and Pasko 2004, 27; Wesely 2006, 305). The ways in which women negotiate instances or potential instances of sexual assault and other forms of personal injury are directly influenced by structural inequalities like gender, race, and class oppression. These factors combine to further complicate the daily lives of young women, including how they negotiate interpersonal violence. In several cases women react to violent attacks directed toward them by meeting their assailant with violence of their own in the form of self-defense (Wesely 2006).

Though some women have used violence as a successful form of self-defense when being threatened by an attacker, Hollander (2009) found mixed reactions from participants of whether or not they believe formal self-defense training strengthens a woman's ability to resist. In evaluation research more broadly, self-defense training has proven to be a strong intervention in preventing stranger violence against women specifically sexual violence. Yet Hollander found in her study three forms of resistant reactions by participants regarding women engaging in formal self-defense training. The first is the "impossible" reaction, which states that it is impossible for women in general to physically overpower a male attacker, even though research has shown that nearly 75 percent of intended rape victims fight off their assailant or escape. The second reaction is that self-defense training is "too dangerous"; the idea here is that formal training will encourage women to enter potentially dangerous situations because they believe they can defend themselves as well as begin to violently attack men. This reaction implies that women are not rational enough to judge when and where to put their self-defense training to use. The third reaction to women's formal self-defense training is "victim blaming," which implies that women are responsible for protecting themselves against assault and also responsible for controlling the violence of attackers. Though women cannot control men's violence and should not be held responsible to do so, formal self-defense training has proven to be an effective form of deterrence for men and personally empowering for women. These three reactions represent mainstream cultural ideas about gender and, in particular, they reinforce ideas about women being weak and irrational. Self-defense challenges the ideas that many people see as "natural," thus challenging extant gendered hierarchies (Hollander 2009).

For the women in the present study, formal self-defense training is a luxury that is unavailable. These women develop their own strategies to negotiate MIAs with men on the street. They have learned to manage daily encounters where their personal safety is at risk by developing their own methods of defense while living with feelings of fear and vulnerability. This already complicated project is intensified by distressed community conditions. These women are at tremendous risk for personal injury in the inner city; each day they must work to negotiate their safety, which is not guaranteed.

EVERYDAY ENCOUNTERS WITH STREET-BASED MICROINTERACTIONAL ASSAULTS

Street-based MIAs described in this chapter are different from consumer-oriented MIAs in a number of ways. First, these interactional exchanges occur outside the boundaries of local businesses. The experiences associated with consumer-oriented assaults are largely contained by the physical boundaries of the establishment in which they occur, although the resultant social injury is often carried with a person beyond these physical boundaries. Different from harassment, street-based MIAs highlight the role of violence within these interactions. Once on the street in East Oakland, there are limited physical barriers between persons. In addition, the code of civility that can be a part of interactions that unfold inside businesses does not apply in the same way to street encounters. The form of public courtesy that is expected to operate on the street is what Erving Goffman calls "civil inattention." This form of visual recognition of another's presence is designed to display a casual and brief appreciation of the other in this space without showing any special curiosity (1963, 83–88). Women in the neighborhood experience violations of this expectation of civil inattention in the form of street-based MIAs. Such violations occur repeatedly, and the belief that civil law will not provide adequate protection makes these women particularly vulnerable on the street.

Here the street is primarily regulated by what Elijah Anderson (1999) notes is the "code of the street." Behavior on the part of many who live in the inner city is governed by the threat of violence or confrontation. For women, in particular, behavior is often influenced by the threat of physical as well as sexual violence. The second way in which street-based MIAs differ from consumer-oriented MIAs is that for women these street-based encounters typically involve sexual harassment and threats of sexual violence. My respondents' accounts and observations include cases of name-calling, physical violence, and unwanted sexual invitation.

The following account from Shante, a woman in her early twenties, illustrates a common way in which street-based MIAs occur. I asked Shante what kinds of experiences she has had with men on the street, and she described how men approach her as she walks through East Oakland:

> Typically, when I am walking down the street around here guys act like dogs. They yell "Hey girl" to get me to turn around, but if I ignore them they start calling me all out of my name [derogatory name calling]. It happens all the time. It's like they're always saying something foul; if it's at least two of them out on the corner, then you know they probably got something to say to you. It don't matter what you're doing or if you're just going about your business. They either hollering about how they want to "get with

you," or if you reject them, they talk all kinds of shit about you and why you are just a bitch just 'cause you don't want them.

Shante's account illustrates how women don't have to be engaged in a traditional one-on-one interaction in order to be a target of forceful male behavior in public; just being present in urban public space as a woman managing multiple categorical identities is enough to be singled out and treated aggressively. The type of interaction that Shante describes is common for women in the inner city. Such interactions generally unfold as three steps in one of two scenarios: as *invitation–refusal of invitation–escalation*, or as *invitation–acceptance of invitation–civil public interaction.*

The encounter begins with an invitation. In Shante's case, the men on the street began to yell "Hey girl" in an effort to gain her attention. Other types of invitations include verbalizing evaluations of women such as "You really wearing that dress" or "You're too pretty to be out here standing at the bus stop." Some invitations are also physical, like grabbing a woman's arm as she walks down the street. Each form of invitation is intended to catch the attention of the woman targeted and is commonly followed by a refusal. In this case, Shante chose to refuse the invitation by ignoring the men's advance. Often women in this setting refuse invitations by men they don't know, just as Shante did. But some cases show women engaging in what appears to be casual conversation with men who approach them on the street. This is considered an acceptance of the invitation. In turn, the acceptance results in what appears to be a causal conversation, also a form of civil public interaction. Finally, it is significant to note that there is always a level of unpredictability within such interactions. As a result, some street-based MIAs may unfold in a less predictable manner than those reflected in the patterns described here.

More commonly, invitations are met with refusals that take the form of a woman ignoring both the request and the men extending the invitation by quickly walking away from the space or averting the gaze of those trying to gain notice. Once a refusal of an invitation occurs, the interaction often begins to escalate. Escalation routinely takes the form of verbal disputes where yelling and name-calling are central. Verbal escalation may be initiated by either party and is sometimes engaged in by both. Shante described how this particular interaction began to escalate in response to her refusal. At this point the men began to verbally assault her with derogatory names; she continued to refuse their initial invitation by not verbally engaging in the interaction. The escalation seems to gain momentum when there is more than one man in the audience, as the presence of other male friends or acquaintances seems to encourage the progression of this type of interaction. In these types of cases it is significant for some young men to prove their manhood to others—both to peers and any women present—by asserting their male dominance. This can take the form of brutal name-calling, such as referring to the woman as "bitch," "ho," or "freak" or through physical violence, such as grabbing the body parts of the woman targeted. The presence of a small group works to reinforce the dominant male status of the men involved in the interaction while magnifying the woman's subordinate female status. With the presence of other men this encounter becomes more than a one-on-one interaction; it develops into a kind of interactional performance in which others can become a part, escalating it either verbally or physically, or simply bearing witness as the interaction unfolds. Finally, in the cases where women outnumber a man, initiating an invitation can escalate to the point of physical violence. In these encounters some women have aggressively refused invitations and further responded by attacking the man and engaging in a public beating. Usually in cases like this the man is significantly older than the women targeted and is assumed to pose less of a physical threat than a much younger man.

The following case of a one-on-one interaction unfolds in the same pattern as the encounter Shante described. Tiffany, a young woman, described an episode she had with a man on the street that began with an invitation, was followed by her refusal, and concluded with an escalation. This interaction began as Tiffany exited a neighborhood store carrying baby formula; as she prepared to cross the street, a shiny blue sedan screeched to a stop before her and abruptly interrupted her path. Tiffany stared angrily at the driver suddenly blocking her pathway, and she noted the big smile on his face when he exited his car and approached her as she tried to walk away:

> I just tried to ignore him, the way he was looking at me was like I was naked or something. He kept saying, "You with the big booty, I want to talk to you," but I just kept on walking. Then he called me a ho with a fucked-up attitude, and I got really hot [angry], but then I was just like, forget it, it ain't even worth it. I was so mad 'cause he doesn't even know me and he thinks it's okay to talk about my ass to my face like that. The twisted thing is he thinks it's a compliment, but then if I don't act like I like it I got to be a ho with a fucked-up attitude.

In this encounter the man used his vehicle as a way to initiate an invitation. By blocking Tiffany's path across the street, her movement was stalled, and this allowed him the opportunity to follow up with a verbal invitation demanding that she talk to him. The use of a vehicle as a physical barrier restricting the young woman's mobility even for a moment, complicated by the stranger making demands of her, symbolize ways in which gendered inequality manifests in daily interactions on the street. Tiffany rejected the invitation by ignoring the man and his demands. Her act of ignoring his demands is a form of resistance to his harassment. This refusal prompted an escalation where the man verbally assaulted her with offensive speech and name-calling. His reaction is a lived consequence of her rejection to this unwanted behavior.

This interaction was surely rooted in some troubling assumptions about gender. Tiffany, like all women who negotiate public space, shared a sense of vulnerability. Yet because she is young, Tiffany did not experience the protection that can come with being of an older age and considered less sexually available. In addition, she was not guarded by the privilege that can accompany a higher social status than the working-class standing that she claims. The man in the encounter seemed to understand Tiffany in the context of black female promiscuity. In her refusal to take part in this script, and in her rejection of his expression of hyper-heterosexual masculinity, the escalation intensified (Collins 2005, 115). The verbal assault worsened, but in an effort to keep the escalation from the point of possible physical violence, Tiffany walked away, though infuriated.

Black gender ideologies that replicate dominant racist ideas about what it means to be poor, black, and female play out in troubling ways, as the accounts of experiences shared by Tiffany and Shante illustrate. Both women noted frustration at being called indecent names by men on the street. In response to being called out in this way Shante used rejection as a defensive tool against the men hollering at her. In her account it seems that rejecting the sexual invitations of men, particularly in a public space, was extremely upsetting for them and in their eyes justification to call her a bitch. This back-and-forth interaction resembles a struggle for power in the poor urban neighborhood, where residents are often deemed powerless. The young men who attacked Shante with their words were fighting to bring into being their historically castrated black masculinity. Simultaneously, Shante was fighting her own oppression as a poor black woman subject to abuse; she rejected the attempt at male dominance by putting down the sexual invitation and challenging the young men's heteronormative masculinity. Yet she noted how this "happens all the time." Such oppressive acts imposed upon her black womanhood are routine encounters in this setting (Collins 2005, chap. 7; Jones 2010, chap. 4).

The encounters Tiffany and Shante described are routine in the inner city and reflect Goffman's concept of "regular occasions," which are explained as a unit that grows every time a similar occasion takes place, making the unit a stronger and more familiar cycle of events (1963, 19). In this way MIAs form a blanket of interactional injury in women's lives. Tiffany and Shante illustrate through their experiences how street-based MIAs become regular occasions for women in this setting, a routine component of their daily life.

Tiffany and Shante's experiences also raise questions about the meanings and perceptions of youth, femaleness, blackness, and poverty by others when one is out in public. Tiffany went on to further explain her experience, making clear, "I'm not afraid of anybody, I can't afford to be; but I also can't fight everybody who says or does something out of line to me or else I would be fighting most of the time." One of the troubling elements in these interactions is the expectation that these women will willingly accept the assumption that they are available to the men they encounter. This assumption of availability underscores Collins's idea of asserting and maintaining domination within a culture of rape (2005, chap. 7). The way that the young black man approaches this young black woman on the street is informed by his own experiences of subordinated masculinity. In an effort to reclaim his masculinity he chooses to encounter this woman in a specific way that reinforces how she is often seen through the dominant lens, as the available hypersexual other. One way this is expressed is by making reference to her by her body parts. This stage of the interaction is what I call invitation. At this point actions are displayed to get and maintain the attention of the woman involved. The next step is the refusal. An example of how the refusal can operate is shown in Tiffany challenging the assertion of dominance the man displayed by ignoring him and walking away.

The final stage of this type of interaction is the escalation. This is illustrated when the man involved reacted by calling Tiffany out as a "ho with a fucked-up attitude," using language to further demean her status as a black woman and simultaneously protect his immediately challenged status as a "real man." These encounters show the microlevel operation of controlling images. The women sharing these encounters are in a way being told who they are and who they are not as they simply walk down the street in their own neighborhood. The men trying to get their attention are verbalizing the larger social indoctrination of who they are said to be as young black women living in an urban community. (Collins 2000, chap. 4; Costa Vargas 2006, 23).

Living in a troubled East Oakland neighborhood and managing your daily tasks sends a message to those you encounter about who you are and who you are not. These women are marked as unequal due to their gender, race, class, and age categories and as a result are subject to the availability of men in this space. They become prey to the inappropriate and harmful social behavior and advances of others. For the women whose encounters and accounts are represented in this study, such behavior has become constant and often unavoidable.

Carol Brooks Gardener notes how public harassment of women by men symbolically reinforces male rights and social control without considerable consequence. This type of behavior in public simply underscores and supports women's vulnerability to other social problems like domestic abuse, rape, and sexual harassment in both the public and private spheres. This type of public social abuse of women is common, and many women have come to expect it; and too many men have become well versed in executing it (Gardener 1995, 86–88). This mutual understanding of giving and receiving abuse reinforces the experiences recounted by the women who live in East Oakland, a point illustrated in Shante's portrayal of her interaction with a group of men. When asked about her experiences with men on the street, Shante stated that "guys act like dogs" and then went on to give a description of what men do in interactions with women on the street and how this angers her. She implied that this is the understood way of being for young men in this context, emphasizing that being yelled at and called foul names by male passersby attempting to get her attention occurs routinely, even when she is minding her own business.

The following story recounts nineteen-year-old Kira's experience with street-based MIAs as she walks through Sunnyside each day:

> Every day for the past few weeks I see these same guys on the corner. It's usually three, sometimes four of them at a time. At first when I would walk past them on my way to the bus stop, one of them would be like "Hi, how you doing," "You look good," or "When you gonna give me your (telephone) number?" and I wouldn't say anything, just keep on walking. Then after, like, two weeks of passing them every day, one of the guys seemed to get all angry and one day was like, "You think you too good to talk to me? You ugly anyway." So I still didn't say anything, I just kept walking and ignoring them. Then one day the same guy saw me walking toward them and started talking crazy and was getting loud so I could hear him. He said, "Here come that little stuck-up ho, don't nobody

want your ho ass anyway," and then they all started laughing. So then I couldn't take it no more, so I started yelling and screaming and cussing him out. He just kept saying, "Girl, get out my face; don't make me hit you."

Kira's report displays the routine nature of sexually harassing speech from men in her neighborhood. This interaction is an example of a daily street-based microinteractional assault. Kira described how her interactions with this small congregation of young men in public began to escalate over a period of weeks. After she initially tried to ignore their advances, the encounters become increasingly antagonistic. These men who did not know her, except that she passed them each day, repeatedly made advances toward her. When she responded to their remarks with silence she refuted their attempts at asserting masculinity while their peers looked on. As a result, the comments become increasingly hostile. With each subsequent interaction Kira worked to protect herself from having the encounter turn into an altercation by remaining silent. One of the young men seemed increasingly irritated by her response (or lack thereof). It is likely that he felt his masculine identity being further challenged by Kira's silence. Being in the presence of his peers and struggling to avoid humiliation by this young woman increased his annoyance with her and thus increased his desire to further objectify her and put her down. Finally, one of the young men made a last attempt at displaying his male dominance over Kira and the space she passes through by calling her a "stuck-up ho" whom "nobody wants."

This personal attack ignited Kira's angry reaction: cursing at the man in front of his peers, further injuring his masculine identity. He concluded with a threat, "don't make me hit you." The way in which this threat of violence is made placed Kira at fault if the man hits her. The structure of this remark underscores the presence of female victimization in urban space: as Kira spoke out in her own defense, the young man worked to silence her through a threat of physical violence.

The element of Kira's interaction that makes it different from the earlier cases discussed is that it unfolded continuously over a matter weeks. The encounter follows the pattern of *invitation–refusal–escalation*, though as Kira related, the escalation increased to the point of a threat of physical assault. This is unlike the previous interactions that generally display *invitation–refusal–escalation* in one day during a single interaction, though it is significant to note that like each other case this account illustrates how female subordination is a central component to these routine interactions. This is made visible through routine instances of gender-specific verbal assault.

These types of encounters place black women in a sort of lose–lose situation as they try to negotiate urban public space. If they try to ignore the harassment, it gets worse; and if they call attention to the harasser's behavior by staging a turnabout and deferring the attention back to him, their personal safety is put in jeopardy. The fragility of a woman's personal safety in this setting is illustrated in the following account from Nicole, a twenty-one-year-old mother of a two-year-old daughter. I asked Nicole if she has had any encounters with men in the neighborhood who appear older than her, and she told me of an encounter with a middle-aged black man while she waited at a bus stop in her East Oakland neighborhood. "It was early one morning in the winter," she explained. "The weather was cold and raining and it was still dark outside. I was holding my daughter as we stood in this doorway trying to stay dry. This man who looked old enough to be my father was walking by and slowed down to say, 'You are too pretty to be out here by yourself this time of morning. A man like me could take you in that alley and tear you up [sexually assault you].' He shook his head and smiled as he walked away."

Nicole described this encounter as "scary," adding, "The worst part about it is that I felt trapped. I was holding my daughter, who was asleep; it was raining and dark and it wasn't like I could scream and someone would do something, because there was no one around." Nicole's feelings of being trapped and scared are a direct reaction to the threats made by a man as he passed her on the street. These threats symbolize his dominant male status in this local street hierarchy. Nicole later explained to me that she responded to this man's remarks with silence out of fear of making the situation worse. She mentioned how she was trying to think of how to get away from him if she had to, while keeping her daughter safe. Nicole described an intuitive understanding of how rejection leads to escalation. Simultaneously, her daughter is being socialized into what it means to be a poor black girl in this setting. Nicole described how, after the man walked away, she "sort of froze" at the thought of what could have happened to her and her child. Her encounter with a strange man on the street is certainly a threatening one. Her personal safety and that of her young child were at risk at that moment. Further, the man insinuated that if she were in this same circumstance again, a man like him could "tear her up." This interaction is an example of a street-based microinteractional assault that is informed by the threat of sexual violence. With each interaction the role of women as the "devalued other" is intensified (Collins 2005, 187). As the re-creation of this subordinated status through daily interactions occurs repeatedly, hegemonic masculinity is reinforced. Women trying to manage daily tasks in disadvantaged communities must often struggle to do so, in part because of experiences of routine microassaults. It is assaults like this one, in addition to the types of MIAs discussed in chapter 2, that make negotiating already troubled circumstances even more challenging and dangerous. This interaction is a reminder of how inner-city neighborhoods are governed by the "code of the street" (Anderson 1999). Events like this highlight the gendered dimensions of the code: that men primarily worry about physical violence while women must contend with the threat of physical violence *and* sexual violence as they navigate urban public space each day.

CONTROLLING IMAGES AND GENDERED VIOLENCE

In Collins's (2000) discussion of controlling images as they relate to black women's oppression, she points out how widely accepted stereotypical images like the sexually aggressive whore and the welfare queen are designed to make multiple forms of oppression seem natural and expected parts of daily life. As racism, poverty, sexism, and other social injustices prevail, so does this othering of black women. It is this "other" status that clarifies the boundaries by which dominant groups define what is normal and what is not. Controlling images are one of the most significant tools at work in daily interactions and larger social institutions; these images invoke degrading stereotypes that are used to substantiate the imposed marginalization of oppressed groups.

Previous research on gender and public harassment has revealed the harsh reality of public space for those who are situationally disadvantaged. Public space belongs to everyone and no one simultaneously (Gardener 1995). It is a place that is theoretically civil to all people but in reality a place where many are ridiculed and put down. It is here where people experience threats of violence, injury, and rejection. Evidence shows that not everyone receives equal treatment (Gardener 1995, 44). Specifically, in underserved neighborhoods where resources are often severely limited, the situation can increase the struggle of managing threatening encounters for the black women who live there.

In her study on African American girls, urban inequality, and gendered violence, Jody Miller describes gender "as a structural, interactional, and symbolic source of inequality" (2008, 2). Miller highlights how gender is rarely portrayed or understood in this way. In the Unites States, where violence against women and girls is systematic, Miller points out how this reality is even more severe in our nation's disadvantaged communities. East Oakland, a predominantly black distressed community, is similar to poor inner-city neighborhoods throughout the United States. The women who live in Sunnyside do their best to negotiate this troubled environment each day as they receive little or no institutional or social support. The services and support systems that are available prove to be largely insufficient in keeping women safe. With poor communities comes the long history of raced and classed oppression that impacts men, women, and children. As a result, underground networks of prostitution, drug sales, gang affiliations, and other forms of alternative work that often prove to be unsafe spring up in many communities. Many become forced into these networks after being isolated from mainstream employment opportunities that produce a livable wage.

For some young men living in troubled urban neighborhoods, being a part of this type of alternative workforce can operate as a way of developing and performing masculinity. Here street reputation has a lot to do with their masculine identity construction. Creating a masculine street reputation that garners respect from peers is significant for many young men; developing this type of self-presentation means displaying an image of toughness, independence, willingness to use violence, and heterosexual expertise illustrated through sexual conquest (Anderson 1999). Many young women become subject to degradation and street harassment as young men work to build a masculine identity and local status. Much of this street work is directly linked to the visible objectification of and violence against women, including verbal, physical, and intimate partner abuse. The organizational characteristics of urban street networks often produce gender inequality. The majority of this work, specifically in the leadership roles of pimp, drug dealer, hustler, and the like, is male dominated. For the women living in communities with active underground networks public space can be complicated and often unsafe to navigate from day to day. It appears that severe poverty within disadvantaged neighborhoods is what structures the high risk for gendered violence that African American young women experience.[1]

STRATEGIES OF RESISTANCE

Troubled interactions on the street further complicate managing inner-city life for many black women. Every day, women must make a choice of how to negotiate these kinds of encounters— through avoidance, engagement, or resistance, with the latter shown to be common. Resistance is a contributing factor in how many MIAs unfold. Two essential features of resistance are action and opposition. These overt forms of counteraction are intentional on the part of the actor and recognized by the target. Resistance is fundamentally interactional and defined by an actor's perception of her own behavior as well as by the recognition and reaction of the target. When considering how resistance operates, it is crucial to point out the central role of power in interactions where resistance takes place (Hollander and Einwohner 2004, 547–548). When negotiating MIAs with men on the street, my respondents repeatedly work to resist dominant race, gender, and classed ideologies as well as power dynamics that frame this type of interaction and the real threats to their well-being.

Two primary tactics employed by women to negotiate and defend against street-based MIAs are interactional resistance and buffering. *Interactional resistance* is the verbal or physical confrontation or opposition to a microinteractional assault and to the person(s) carrying it out. Interactional resistance is the larger strategic category that encompasses buffering.

Buffering is a form of interactional resistance that includes both physical and psychological shielding against interactional pain, discomfort, and hostility. Although buffering is not intended to be as confrontational as interactional resistance, both approaches are grounded in self-defense as a response to street harassment. The action of buffering works to reduce the impact of uneasy interactions without initiating an aggressive conflict. Psychological buffering can consist of normalizing a situation or behavior—for instance, telling oneself "it happens all the time" or "that's just the way it is." Physical buffering can take the form of physically shielding one's body from an interactional assault or verbally defending oneself in a way that generally reflects civil public interaction. While buffering reflects what some describe as avoidance, what I conceptualize as physical buffering can involve women using local convenient stores and takeout restaurants as physical barriers between themselves and potentially troubling public encounters. Interactional resistance more broadly includes verbally admonishing the actions and/or words used by one person to assault another. This form of verbal resistance can easily escalate to a physical dispute, which can in turn also be an act of interactional resistance. In this study I observe both physical, and more commonly, verbal confrontations in response to MIAs.

The forms of resistance that women take up are acts of self-preservation; they work to resist and buffer oneself from routine MIAs as an intrinsic form of physical and emotional protection. Yet there are consequences to such resistance. In many cases women are in a lose-lose situation. Though opposition to MIAs is common, these incidents still occur repeatedly. In some cases resistance can worsen the level of escalation in an interaction, causing a greater threat of personal injury. This includes opening women up to intensified verbal assault and the threat and/or act of physical and sexual violence. Acts of resistance defy mainstream gendered expectations of women and girls to submit to male dominance, and defying such expectations results in punishment. The process of *expectation–violation–punishment* is a routine element of these daily MIAs. Each time this series of actions takes place, dominant gender ideologies and inequality are reproduced.

Interactional Resistance

Women verbally and sometimes physically defend themselves when engaged in street-based MIAs. Some of the defensive acts they perform include cursing, yelling, name-calling, pushing, and hitting. The following excerpt from my field notes shows how a girl in her mid-teens performs interactional resistance while waiting at a bus stop:

> I observe from a short distance as a young girl waits patiently at the bus stop. She leans her body against the metal pole where the bus schedule is posted. As she waits, I observe her reading a book. Periodically she looks up from the pages and glances around, then goes back to her book. As she reads, I notice two teenage boys walking down the street in her direction. One of the boys swings a plastic soda bottle in one hand as he walks and talks to the boy beside him. As they get closer to where the girl stands, the boy with the soda bottle puts his index finger over his lips indicating to his friend to be quiet as they reach the bus stop. The teenage girl is looking down at her book when the boy hits the girl on her butt with the soda bottle as he passes by. Almost instantly the girl turns and punches the boy in the arm, and he laughs in response. "Damn girl, I was just playing," he says.
>
> "You think you funny, James, and you're not. I'm not playing with you. Do it again and see what happens," the girl replies.

"Man, whatever. Bitches be trippin'," the boy says to his friend, who nods his head in agreement but remains quiet as they walk away.

When the boy gets the teenage girl's attention by touching her inappropriately, she immediately confronts his behavior with both physical and verbal acts of interactional resistance: she hits the boy in the arm and dares him to repeat the behavior to "see what happens." As she defends herself in this way the boy quickly retorts in his own defense that he was "just playing." Though the boy does not physically retaliate after she hits him and challenges him to "do it again," he reacts by saying "bitches be trippin'," thus referring to her as a bitch. It seems that though he doesn't really want to fight this girl physically, he does want to save face while maintaining his sense of masculine identity, particularly in front of his friend. The boy goes about saving face by asserting that the girl is a bitch because she didn't like, or passively accept, him violating her body and personal space by touching her inappropriately. Miller points out that within the context of sexually violent behavior, women experience very gender-specific risks in public, and their experiences of violence and harassment can and often do take on characteristics of "public spectacle" (2008, 35). The interaction of the girl and the boy at the bus stop becomes a spectacle of sorts, as it is a troubled interaction including unwanted touching, name-calling, and argumentative responses on public display for all passersby to see. This type of interaction illustrates how street-based MIAs are "regular" occasions (Goffman 1963, 19) that sometimes, but not always, take on the form of spectacle.

The teenage girl in this interaction acknowledges that the boy who wrongfully touches her while on the street is "playing" and is trying to be "funny." A part of her verbal form of interactional resistance makes this known while at the same time plainly stating that his efforts to be funny were unsuccessful and in no way does she accept his acts as playfulness. A part of the teenage boy being able to explain away his behavior as a joke that should be happily accepted reinforces his dominant male status within the system of gendered street hierarchy—a hierarchy that places women subordinate to men and keeps them situationally disadvantaged (Miller 2008, 39). This *less than* status experienced by women and girls is largely accepted by men on the streets of distressed inner-city communities, underscoring the assumed sexual availability of women and girls in such a setting. The teenage boy's assertion that this girl is a "bitch" illustrates that he has made an evaluation of who she is during the encounter. This oppressive evaluation is informed by her rejection of him inappropriately touching her body while in public. In addition, dominant perceptions of her categorical identities, including race, class, and gender, further inform evaluations made about who she is—in this interaction and beyond. Without social and legal services in place to help minimize cases of street harassment and street-based sexual violence, they will persist. The following account by Angel, an 18-year-old high school student, describes how she employs interactional resistance when a middle-aged man approached her and two of her friends as he was smoking outside a local bar one weekday afternoon:

> Me and two of my friends were walking home and we passed Doug's Lounge—it's this grimy bar or whatever. This old man—like, fifties—was outside smoking a cigarette. He was smiling and showing his missing teeth on the side of his mouth. Anyway, as we was walking by he goes, "Hey ladies, what y'all doing later tonight?"
> "Not talking to you," I said.

"Oh I like that, you gotta smart mouth and a fast ass. You, come over here and let daddy show you what he gon' put in your smart mouth."

I was like, oh hell no, I am not the one, so me and my girls all looked at each other and then we rushed his dirty old ass. We started punching him and kicking him till he was on the ground. He started screaming "Stop, stop!" and then some people from the bar came out and pulled us off of him. But I didn't care, 'cause we got him good, and he deserved it.

In this account Angel illustrates the role of escalation in the interaction. We see what began as an unwanted advance develop into a threat of sexual assault. Angel's account depicts a rare encounter of women using physical aggression in retaliation, an act that violates norms of femininity. Interactional resistance is performed here both verbally and physically. First, Angel refuses the man's initial advance, which he appears to be using as both a question—"Hey ladies, what y'all doing tonight?"—and an informal invitation. Angel quickly replies, "Not talking to you," which implies that she and her friends are not interested in talking to him at the time of question or at any other time. The man seems put off by Angel's sharp reply, and reacts by making an evaluation of her. He states that she has a "smart mouth," which she doesn't seem overly bothered by. Yet it is the evaluation of her being a "fast ass," insinuating that she is promiscuous, followed by a threat of a sexually violent act, that prompts her and her friends to physically attack him. The order in which the evaluation and then the threat are made is significant. Some informing components that help this man make a swift evaluation of who Angel is include her race, class, gender, and social location in addition to her sharp reply to his advance, determining for him that she is both hypersexual and deserving of threats of sexual violence.

At the moment Angel and her friends attack their perpetrator physically, the gender hierarchy becomes inverted
through the form of retaliation or street justice that the girls
take up. Yet as the young women use physical aggression as a
way of defending themselves from verbal assault and threats of
sexual assault, they also reinforce stereotypes about poor black
women: the aggression they exhibit exemplifies dominant
ideas about the violent and impulsive angry black woman
(Logan 2011). The lived outcomes of such oppressive evaluations can make managing daily life in inner-city communities
even more complicated than it already is for the black women
who live in them.

Buffering

Traveling in and out of distressed urban neighborhoods is
complicated for female residents. One of the ways in which
they negotiate and manage routine street-based MIAs is through
buffering. Both physical and psychological buffering work to
assist them in maintaining safety while negotiating daily travel
and residence in the inner-city space. Twenty-year-old Amaya
describes one way in which she routinely employs physical buffering as she travels through the East Oakland neighborhood
where she lives: "When I walk down Third Avenue, I try to
always be with somebody else. During the day it's not too bad.
The guys hanging outside do say nasty stuff and try to be slick
and touch you when you go by, but at night or really early in
the morning that's when it's rough out here. That's when girls
get snatched up." In this account, Amaya tells of how she tries
to stay safe as she walks through her neighborhood each day.
She describes using physical buffering by not walking along this
street alone. Amaya employs Gardener's concept of adopting
strategic protectors as a way of buffering herself from unwanted
encounters with men on the street. Gardener proposes that
appearing in public places with a companion may discourage

harassment (1995, 206–208). Amaya explains that not being alone when passing men on this street helps to keep her safe from what she describes as being "snatched up" or from more severe sexual assaults. The local understanding of being "snatched up" alludes to kidnapping and forced prostitution; the threat of both structures women's' daily lives. In the street, accompaniment may prevent some—but not all—inappropriate remarks or unwanted touching.

A significant component of Amaya's experience with street-based MIAs is that she has ranked the different types of microinteractional assaults that she is familiar with in this community and has evaluated them based on what she understands to be more or less dangerous. In a casual tone she mentions that during the day, when primarily inappropriate comments and touching occur, it's "not too bad." She is, however, regularly reminded of her subordinate status as she is subjected to unwanted touching and remarks when walking through her neighborhood. She goes on to describe that cases of being "snatched up" or severely sexually assaulted demonstrate when it is "rough out here." It is critical for Amaya and other black women in inner-city communities to be keenly aware of their surroundings—including when, where, and how different kinds of MIAs take place—in an effort to ensure their own personal safety. Nevertheless, it is important to note that such ranking is also a form of psychological buffering. Amaya has chosen to protect herself from these troubled encounters in two ways. First, she does not walk alone; this is an act of physical buffering. Second, she tells herself that these daytime assaults are not nearly as bad as the late night or early morning attacks. This type of psychological buffering operates to better help Amaya negotiate unavoidable daily travel through her neighborhood.

It is important to consider the popular notion that members of situationally disadvantaged groups should "be smart" and stay away from areas where they are treated badly; if they don't, they must be asking for trouble (Gardener 1995, 76). Unfortunately this widely accepted notion does not account for the many people who don't have the luxury of living, shopping, and working somewhere else. It does not allow for the reality that many members of situationally disadvantaged groups are treated poorly in most places. Amaya's account reinforces the routine nature of street-based MIAs in this space by showing how women must begin to prioritize when, where, and how to stay safe based on the severity of different kinds of street based MIAs that occur here.

The following excerpt from my field notes illustrates how a teenage girl physically shields her body from the unwanted gaze of an interaction with a male stranger as she waits at a bus stop. It also illustrates how the girl resists a troubled street encounter by removing herself from the immediate site and shielding herself with the company of adults nearby:

> A girl who appears to be in her early teens sits on a bus bench with her book bag next to her. She wears a purple T-shirt, blue jeans, and black flip-flops as she is visibly distracted by whatever appears on the screen of her cell phone. I notice her glance up from her phone once or twice in the direction from where the bus usually comes. I stand a few feet from where the girl sits and notice a middle-aged black man with a medium brown complexion and graying hair. He wears a navy blue zip-up sweatshirt, black pants, and matching black shoes. As he walks toward the bus bench where the girl sits, I see him slightly grin through his full beard. The man slows as he approaches the bus stop. The girl quickly looks up as the man's shadow hovers over where she sits. Seemingly a bit startled, she grabs her book bag and cradles it in her lap. The middle-aged man then sits down on the bench just inches from the girl. I notice the man talking to the girl in a hushed tone

not loud enough for me to hear. As he leans in and continues to talk to her she begins to nervously look around. Still talking, the man moves closer to the girl and stretches his arm out over the back of the bench just inches from her shoulders. The girl looks angrily at the man but remains silent. She promptly stands up, looking away from him, though he turns his head to follow her with his eyes. The young girl walks away from the bench, still holding her book bag in her arms. She steps into the shallow doorway of an abandoned storefront and stands behind a woman, who looks to be in her thirties and is talking on a cell phone, while I stand just a few steps away on her right side.

The young girl described in this encounter demonstrates an act of physical buffering in which she uses her personal belongings as a way to shield herself from an undesired interaction on the street. Upon encountering a middle-aged man at a bus stop she quickly picks up her backpack and holds it in her lap using it to create a physical barrier between herself and a stranger. Eventually the girl stands up and walks away from the bench to find another place to wait for the bus to arrive. In an effort to reclaim a sense of comfort and safety, she places herself between two adult women who are also waiting for the bus; repositioning herself here provides distance from the man on the bench. She then places herself in such a way that she uses the bodies of the two other people present to help shield herself from further interaction with this man. Though the young girl doesn't leave the site after experiencing a troubled interaction, she uses the space available to buffer herself from an already uncomfortable and potentially threatening encounter. The man has used his dominant status as both male and middle-aged to intimidate a teenaged girl. As I illustrated in the opening to this chapter, in this setting a black woman or girl alone is vulnerable; she is often an opportunity for another's predatory behavior.

The next account, by nineteen-year-old Shameeah, explains how she and some of her friends use local businesses as shields from street-based MIAs :

> Me and some of my homegirls don't even deal with all that wild shit the boys around here do. Like, when I'm waiting for the bus over on Fortieth and Main Street it's this group of guys, like four of 'em, and they want to talk about every girl that walks by. Like, "Oooh girl, when we gon' fuck?" and it's, like, I don't even know you. Why you gotta' talk crazy to me? For what? So me and my girls, if we see them coming we just go into the liquor store or the Chinese food place or somewhere and wait for the bus in there. They won't come in there with all that, 'cause if we start fighting in the store the people will call the police.

Shameeah describes a specific way she and her friends use physical buffering as a strategy. Upon seeing a particular group of young men who routinely hang around Fortieth and Main Street—a place she travels through often—she and her friends have begun to use local stores and takeout restaurants as protective barriers against street-based MIAs. This type of buffering reflects what Nikki Jones describes as situational avoidance: the work girls do to avoid potentially threatening situations and social settings (2010, 54). In addition, the girls in this account use the physical presence of store owners and employees to deter these young men from entering and engaging them in face-to-face interactions. According to Shameeah, the threat of the police being called in response to a potentially confrontational interaction inside a store or restaurant seems to keep the young men from following her and her friends. A significant component to Shameeah's use of local businesses as

a part of shielding herself from these assaults is the requirement to patronize these establishments: store owners yell at
people who enter their places of business and hang around for
more than a few minutes without buying anything, telling
them to get out of their stores. In turn, it is likely that Shameeah
and others are expected and often required to make a purchase
to be allowed to stay inside the store while waiting for the bus.
Being required to pay for this type of shielding in an effort to
stay safe is not reasonable; for many women, this is not something they can afford on a daily basis.

Shameeah seems confident in how she and her friends have
creatively used local establishments as a resource to stay safe, a
practical means to physically buffer themselves from street-
based harassment. Yet for some black women living in the
inner city this is not a viable option. Not all people, not even
paying customers, are allowed to use small businesses as temporary waiting areas. Differences in presentation of self (Goffman 1959) can work for or against some women when they are
or are not afforded this resource. There are markers that Shameeah and others present that indicate to some local store
owners that she is the kind of person who is *acceptable* to have
wait in their store (Feagin and Sikes 1994, chap. 2). Shameeah
protects herself from street-based MIAs, and their accompany-
ing magnification, by using local businesses as a barrier, yet
once inside local stores and takeout restaurants her race, class,
gender, and social location keep her under a different type of
surveillance: the hypersurveillance often performed by store
owners and employees upon young black shoppers in urban
communities.

What might typically be described as sexual harassment I
explicitly conceptualize as a form of gendered violence: a street-
based microinteractional assault that follows common patterns
of initiation and escalation. Through understanding how such

assaults unfold and the ways distressed local conditions help shape these interactions, much is revealed about the daily lives of women in the inner city. We see how much is at risk for women who experience these routine instances of public harassment from day to day. In this chapter, I have explored how poor black women feel about this threatening and potentially violent feature of their daily lives and shown how they negotiate these types of events while trying to maintain their own personal safety. The narrative accounts presented here illustrate how women occupying public space are vulnerable in societies where gender is constructed in relation to power, making men dominant and women subordinate. With every instance of street harassment women's inferior status is reinforced and they are routinely reminded of their constant vulnerability to sexual violence and other forms of physical harm (Tuerkheimer 1997, 11–12).

There are physical, emotional, and structural risks and implications to street-based microinteractional assaults. This includes the risk of physical harm and the long-term emotional impact of such violations to one's person. Structural implications include the reinforcement of gendered subordination of women in instances of public harassment and the simultaneous support of men's right to largely define these situations (Gardener 1995, chap. 4). In particular, the implications of street harassment experienced by black women reinforces their position as subordinate within the context of hegemonic gender ideology between groups and maintains their marginalized status within black gender ideology. Through experiences of street harassment in the neighborhood, black women experience a very public form of oppression and domination at the hands of black men. Such acts work to preserve the gender hierarchy within their own race and social class groups (Collins 2005, 185–188).

Deirdre Davis suggests that the street becomes a key forum that maintains and reinforces the gender hierarchy through acts of street harassment (1994, 5). Davis argues that these incidents work to gender the street in four ways. The first is through *exclusion*, because through these acts of male-to-female harassment the street becomes marked as a male space where women are not equal participants in public life and in turn excluded. The second is through *domination*, where men establish and control the boundaries that define women's participation in this space. The third is through *invasion*, as women's right to privacy is invaded by this form of public aggression. And the fourth is through *oppression*, as women's mobility and range of motion are restricted and they are left with an absence of choices regarding when, where, and how to maneuver through this public space, further perpetuating female subordination (Davis 1994, 5–6).

This chapter has illustrated how women can become targets of verbal, physical, and sexually predatory male behavior in the public space of a poor inner-city community. We see how women's subordination is constantly being reinforced as they experience oppressive public encounters with men on the street. I have made central how the impact of these events is intensified for poor black women living in socially isolated communities; these women experience street-based MIAs as "regular occasions" (Goffman 1963, 19) that are folded into the rhythm of their daily lives. Poverty and limited local resources help shape the few options women have for avoiding or exiting community spaces where they are regularly exposed to MIAs. Additionally, if settings where expectations that civil law will protect residents are not trusted, this only increases women's vulnerability to public abuse. Not having reliable forms of protection and support such as civil law and social resources aimed at improving quality of life, poor women in urban settings are likely to remain susceptible to public harassment on the street. It is important to note, however, that because most of these troubled encounters occur on the street in a poor neighborhood regularly exposed to violence, in a safer space women's experiences with these kinds of assaults might decrease. I am hopeful that some will escape this environment and much of the tragedy that occurs within it. But I am aware that their status as black women, poor or not, marks them as a raced and gendered other within the larger U.S. social order that continues to open them up to verbal, physical, and sexual assault in a variety of settings.

CHAPTER 4

"Keeping It Fresh"

SELF-REPRESENTATION AND
CHALLENGING CONTROLLING
IMAGES IN THE INNER CITY

FOR MANY BLACK women, living in an inner-
city community means living in a place that lacks many of
the resources that are available in middle-class neighborhoods.
This includes grocery stores as well as a variety of retail
shops, banks, and other businesses and services. Managing
daily life in a place where such resources are missing requires
creativity on the part of the people who live there. The strategy of "keeping it fresh" is a result of such creativity. Women
in the inner city use available material resources to challenge
common expectations that tend to complicate their encounters
with others. Through their daily self-presentation these women
illustrate how the aesthetic performance of keeping it fresh works
as a preventive approach used to buffer oneself from microinteractional assaults. As they challenge prevailing ideas about what it
looks like to be poor, black, and female in the inner city—for
example, by carefully crafting their style of dress and their
deportment—they also aim to keep at bay the hostile public
encounters that are often triggered by markers of their class
status. Masking this status is crucial, as they still must manage
their stigmatized categorical identities of race and gender.

What is the meaning of self-presentation for women living in the inner city? How and why do gender, impression management, systemic inequality, and the underground marketplace work together to inform how these women present themselves with regard to physical appearance? Keeping it fresh allows women to present a version of self that aims to achieve particular ends. Depending upon the audience, this strategy also operates as a means of gaining respect and recognition as something other than poor and in some instances works as form of class passing, if only for a moment.

Women in East Oakland rely on informal retail sale and trade systems in their local communities in an effort to keep it fresh. Goods purchased via the underground marketplace allow these women to maintain a neat appearance enhanced by expensive clothes, shoes, and accessories, which challenges dominant expectations of what it looks like to be poor, black, and female. What does it means to look "good" versus looking "poor," and what struggles come with both? My respondents told of the desire to be perceived by outsiders as something different, something better than the image that accompanies being poor, black, and female. As many women reported, it feels good to look good. For most of the women in this study, the outcomes of public encounters largely remain the same while keeping it fresh. Yet respondents repeatedly showed that this strategic performance of a particular aesthetic, although not always successful in changing the perceptions and behavior of outsiders, works consistently to help them feel good and that alone makes managing daily public encounters a bit more bearable.

"It's the Only Way to Be"

In East Oakland, women commonly reproduce a locally valued form of femininity by "keeping it fresh," a phrase they use to refer not only to themselves but also to other women, men, and children. Lauren, a twenty-two-year-old mother of a four-year-old girl, shared with me how she sees the particular style of dress she chooses for herself and her daughter each day and what she understands keeping it fresh to mean for herself and those around her. "It's the only way to be," she said with a laugh. "Me and my daughter always stay fly [always look good]. I only get her the freshest shoes and outfits, and her hair is always combed and her hair ties match her clothes everyday. If I stay fresh, she has to keep it fresh too. My sister and my best friend are the same way; they kids keep it fresh, I never see them sporting no garbage. They help keep me on point."

It is not uncommon to see women keeping it fresh in high-end clothing and accessories while standing in line at the local grocery store. Popular items among residents in the neighborhood and the typical costs in the mainstream retail marketplace include True Religion jeans ($200–$400); Nike Air Jordan gym shoes ($85–$250); Ugg boots ($130–$240); and Juicy Couture track suits ($200–$275). These women are likely to be wearing expensive goods while making purchases with an Electronic Benefit Transfer card or waiting to cash a check at the local check-cashing establishment. How do low-income women gain access to these high-end items? The underground marketplace plays a key role in a woman's ability to keep it fresh in this setting. In East Oakland it is not uncommon to see cars pull into the parking areas or onto the front lawns of apartment buildings with trunks full of merchandise for sale; many suspect that the merchandise is stolen. Men sell these goods from their cars; women who sell this merchandise typically do so out of their homes, where they transform small living spaces into retail showrooms. The gendered difference in the locations and presentations of these markets is noteworthy. These specific gender displays work to reproduce the local understanding of what it means to be a female versus a male entrepreneur in the underground marketplace. In the underground marketplace, money, drugs, sex, food stamps, alcohol, and other items can often be exchanged for the latest in designer merchandise for men, women, and children. The informal sale and trade system at work here makes expensive merchandise available to a population generally excluded from the retail segment where such goods normally circulate. This creates a population regularly wearing products specifically unintended for this market based on class and social location. Such commodities are used here as class markers based on their retail and popular value.

RESPECTABILITY

Living in East Oakland for much of my youth, I became familiar with the presence of the local underground marketplace. My first introduction to this system was as a teenager at the home of Ms. Thomas, the mother of my friend Jasmine. Ms. Thomas worked as an administrative assistant at the county hospital by day; in the evening and on weekends she sold what she refers to as "hot" or stolen clothes and other goods out of a spare bedroom she had turned into a display area in her small single-family home. As a teen I spent many hours after school and weekends at Ms. Thomas's home hanging out with Jasmine. During this time I watched clothes, shoes, accessories, and the occasional television or computer being delivered or picked up from her home. I routinely saw Ms. Thomas systematically taking orders for such items only in person, negotiating prices for these goods, and holding a steady client base in her second job as an entrepreneur in the underground marketplace. Ms. Thomas was always very strict about her method of payment. "Cash only and only cash," she would say; no credit or barter was allowed under any circumstances.

Spending time at Ms. Thomas's home I saw the comings and goings of both men and women who sold goods locally as she did. I looked on as they made exchanges of goods to later sell to a particular "contact" or customer that one had and the other did not. Ms. Thomas used to regularly say that she didn't mind exchanging goods with other entrepreneurs, but never with customers. She often complained about losing business because some entrepreneurs in the area allowed customers to pay for goods in a variety of ways other than cash. She criticized others in the industry for increasingly accepting payment for goods in the forms of drugs, food stamps, alcohol, and even sex. Yet in whatever form customers paid for their goods many neighborhood residents came to rely on underground entrepreneurs like Ms. Thomas in order to keep it fresh.

I offer the following excerpt from my field notes as an illustration of one young woman and her infant son wearing the kinds of goods sold from homes like Ms. Thomas's and from cars in the neighborhood. This young mother and son display a "fresh" version of self as they wait in line at the local check cashing business:

> A young woman who looks to be about 19 or 20 years old enters this 24-hour check-cashing business pushing a baby stroller. The woman waits patiently in line for her turn behind two older black men. I observe her style of dress, which stands out in this working-poor community. She wears large black sunglasses on top of her head, holding back her shoulder-length hair, which appears to have just been professionally styled. I notice a brown monogram Gucci baby bag hanging from the handle of the stroller, and the young woman carries a matching belt bag clipped around her waist. She wears a white tank top and tight blue jeans and has two long gold necklaces around her neck. When she leans over to pick up her baby, who begins to cry softly, I see that the infant is wearing blue jeans and a tiny white T-shirt, and both mother and son have on

matching brand new Nike gym shoes. She wears a large diamond ring on her left ring finger and what look to be six diamond encrusted gold bangles on her right arm.

This young woman's accessories, clothing, and jewelry disrupt the dominant image of physical dress for a young black mother entering a check-cashing establishment in a distressed urban neighborhood. She and her infant son are dressed in expensive goods while seeking out a service that is generally reserved for the poor with no bank accounts. Additionally, she is in an urban community riddled with poverty where there are no stores that sell the type of merchandise she is wearing.

Here is another example of a woman and her young daughter keeping it fresh as they exit a local nail salon:

A young woman in her early 20s exits a local nail salon with a little girl who looks just like her and appears to be 3 or 4 years old. They stand just steps away from me as we all wait for the bus to arrive. I notice that the little girl and the woman both wear sandals revealing their freshly painted toes. I notice the little girl wearing skinny jeans, a tiny leather jacket, and child-size sunglasses as she holds her hands out in front of her as she waits, not to ruin her manicure. Her hair is neatly arranged in four braids with bright pink barrettes on the ends that match her sparkly pink sandals. I hear the little girl say to the young woman, "Mommy, pick me up." The woman replies, "I can't; I don't want to mess up our nails." The little girl looks slightly puzzled at first, then looks down at her hands and continues to marvel at her brightly painted fingernails.

While I made observations in East Oakland, encounters like these became routine. At this bus stop the young mother seemed well invested in the appearance of her little girl. The child was wearing a thoughtfully put together and seemingly expensive ensemble; in addition, she just had her nails professionally done though she looked to be younger than five years of age. As they waited for the bus to arrive, I saw some class-based contradictions in this case. These presentations of self for mother and child challenge stereotypes held by others of what black women in a poor inner-city community ought to look like.

Black women also make distinctions about other black women; some of what they are doing here is distinguishing themselves from "ghetto chicks," a derisive label used to describe low-income women whose behavior, beliefs, and demeanor contrast with mainstream and black middle-class expectations of appropriate and respectable femininity (Jones 2010, 99; Thompson and Keith 2004, 58). "Ghetto chicks" is another controlling image that women encounter each day. The mother and daughter were in a troubled urban neighborhood and taking public transportation, yet the presentation of the little girl with regard to dress and appearance suggested that they were not low-income or struggling, as many in the neighborhood were. This type of display can work to challenge stereotypical understandings of being poor, black, and female looks like. In many cases this project of keeping it fresh unfolds in venues almost exclusively populated by the poor; nevertheless, it is important for these mothers that their presentation of style distinguishes them from those recognized as less deserving of respect such as ghetto chicks or the prostitutes and transients who frequently loiter in the area. This woman and her daughter present themselves in a particular way that suggests they are different from much of the population here (Bettie 2003, 50) and should be recognized as such. A part of distinguishing oneself from ghetto chicks through keeping it fresh is marking oneself as someone different, someone deserving of respect. By keeping it fresh a particular type of locally valued form of black femininity is being produced. As women perform this particular form of self-presentation they situate themselves somewhere in between the ghetto chick and a respectable lady. The work of keeping it fresh is an investment in a gender identity generally consistent with mainstream notions of respectable black femininity (Collins 2005).

A common belief is that women dress up primarily to get the attention of men or to compete with other women for men, but the women in this study shared other important motivations for keeping it fresh. For mothers, extending this fresh self-presentation to their children made them feel better as both mother and child appeared to be deserving of recognition and respect whether others knew they were poor or not. A desired outcome of keeping it fresh is this sort of recognition by others, including neighbors, friends, and outsiders. This recognition involves being accountable to a normative standard of middle-class styles of dress and self-presentation as understood locally (Jenness and Fenstermaker 2014, 10). Among an almost exclusively poor population, it is significant for women and girls to distinguish themselves and to be recognized as more than poor even if they are not. This recognition as people deserving of respect, even for a moment, makes this routine work of keeping it fresh worthwhile.

The experience of both being and looking poor is a complicated one. As respondents explained to me, keeping it fresh is important because what is almost as bad as being poor is *looking* poor. As one woman noted, "Yes, many people would probably consider me poor, because I am and I have to live with that every day, but I don't have to look that way."

"So what does *poor* look like?" I asked Tameka, a twenty-year-old lifelong Oakland resident.

"You know, throw-away stuff, donation clothes and no-name sneakers; or if you're lucky, Walmart clothes. The stuff nobody really wants, but has, because it's either that or nothing." Tameka's description of what "poor" looks like echoes the widespread attitude about poor people: that to be poor is to be lazy, ignorant, backward, and just plain not good enough (Callahan 2008, 372). Keeping it fresh works not just to challenge dominant understandings of what raced and gendered poverty looks like but also as a way to achieve recognition as someone deserving of respect, even if only in the short term. Achieving this recognition is about feeling that you are as good as those who actually are of a higher-class status (Edgerton 1993, 138–139). The work of keeping it fresh is in part about avoiding the stigma of poverty, but it is also about gaining rewards associated with "looking" like a person deserving of respect.

WHY "KEEPING IT FRESH?"

The project of keeping it fresh is employed in large part as a response to the class-based stigma that accompanies racialized urban poverty. In his study of welfare in America, Mark Robert Rank found that the majority of the welfare recipients he talked to had developed very calculated strategies through which to protect themselves from the subtle scrutiny that accompanies the status of welfare recipient; he discusses how several women made it a point not to "look like the stereotypical welfare mother" (1994, 139). This includes dressing up in nice clothing and jewelry, shopping late at night, only making purchases from store clerks they know personally, or in some cases sending others to use their food stamps for them. This is all in an effort not to fit the image of a welfare recipient and to thus avoid the constant rudeness and dehumanization often experienced at the hands of checkout personnel (Rank 1994, 137–139).

Keeping it fresh works to help women be recognized as something other than poor. Many people cannot pass for something other than impoverished because others know about this aesthetic performance and how it is commonly used. Others also know that their neighbors are poor regardless of how they dress. Nevertheless, hiding the stigma of poverty, whether it is a secret or not, is important. While passing locally is rarely successful, keeping it fresh operates as a way to be recognized as something other than poor locally. This tactic is employed by black women in an effort to look like those who are deserving of respect based on their presentation of style. Though concealing the stigma of poverty through passing (Jenness and Fenstermaker 2014, 9) is unlikely in the neighborhood, achieving recognition as respected by others in the community can momentarily outshine one's poverty, something that usually takes center stage. Beyond the local community there seems to be another audience where passing is possible: the imagined rest of the world. This audience takes the form of store personnel and others who come to this community but are not considered members of it; these outsiders do not live in the neighborhood, and they are unfamiliar with those who do. Women here can encounter outsiders on the street, in local businesses, and while riding the city bus. Keeping a "fresh" self-presentation supports the work women do to be recognized as respectable even when representing a class status other than poor is not possible.

Keeping it fresh extends previous scholarship and the concepts of *dressing up* and *covering* through its specific connection to the underground marketplace (Kaplan 1997; Rank 1994). This method of masking one's true class status to the outside world while contradicting normative expectations of poor black women through physical appearance and styles of dress would not be nearly as prominent in the East Oakland community without the accessibility of goods provided by the underground marketplace. In the following account Ron and Avis, a middle-aged black couple who worked nine-to-five jobs but also self-identified as "small time hustlers," shared "how it all works." As Avis, a slender woman with a chocolate brown complexion who stood barely five feet tall and wore her salt-and-pepper hair pulled back into a tight ponytail, explained,

Without people like me and my man Ron, most of the people around here would walk around looking like the world expects all of us to look, like nothing 'cause we black and ain't got nothing, really. But we bring nice clothes, shoes, whatever you want right to your door for a good price. Without us or somebody else bringing the goods to you it would be damn near impossible to look good, the way most folks around here are struggling. How I see it, everybody wins. You get the stuff you want but can't normally afford at a discount, and we make a living at the same time. We all are struggling, but at least this way everybody gets something.

Ron, a short round man in his late forties with a cinnamon brown complexion and a bald head, described for me a little about how the pricing system worked for the goods that he and his girlfriend Avis sold out of their van:

Bottom line, everything is negotiable 'cause the point is to sell it as quick as you can, not carry it around. If I have ten boxes of gym shoes that sell in the store for $150, I try to get $50–$60 for a pair. If they want more than one, I may give them two for $80–$85. Or if I have an order and know the size I'm looking for, I may get $600 worth of stuff from a particular store and sell the whole thing to one person for $250–$300. It all depends on the day, what we got, and what we need.

While neither would disclose the ways in which they specifically acquired merchandise, the underground marketplace in East Oakland primarily consists of selling and trading what are often stolen goods to community residents. As longtime East Oakland resident Charles, a black man in his early fifties, made clear when asked about where he thought a lot of the goods came from, "Yeah, the stuff floating around here is stolen. I think pretty much everybody is aware of that. I mean, some of the stuff still has [store] tags on it, and those young people selling it surely didn't sew those clothes or make those toys, I'm sure of that."

Participation in the underground marketplace is one specific entrepreneurial strategy at work within the larger capitalist market. Although this system may impact some specific businesses, it does not undermine capitalism itself, largely because its profits circulate in the greater market. Yet this very particular niche serves inner-city communities with basic wants and needs that are typically unavailable to local residents. As underground entrepreneurs, Ron and Avis explained how goods are made available to those who want to appear to have more disposable income and higher class status than they actually do and described some of what it takes to maintain the sort of appearance that is upheld by those recognized as deserving of respect. For women in East Oakland the work of keeping it fresh is done in the hope of gaining some respect.

Respondents interviewed for this study described experiences purchasing or trading goods from people in the area selling them out of cars or living spaces. One woman stated openly that she did not think of buying or selling these goods as stealing; she thought of it as taking care of her children and herself. She went on to say that the "true robbery" is the retail cost of goods and it is those who create these prices who are the criminals. This claim is complicated by the reality that many retail establishments refuse to open businesses in poor inner-city communities. East Oakland resident Mara, a twenty-three-year-old mother of a newborn son, expressed how she felt about supporting the local underground marketplace. "I don't take the stuff, anyway," she explained. "I just buy it from the guys around here who have it. I mean, I don't have a car to get out of here the way I would like to, but I still want nice things and my baby deserves to have nice things too, even if I can't afford to get them from the store like some people can. Anyway, the people hustling the clothes and stuff over here are just trying to live like the rest of us. I guess in a way we help each other out.

For Mara, keeping it fresh is in part about wanting "nice things," though her lower-class status indicates she is unworthy of them. Many people living within a consumer capitalist culture desire nice things just as Mara does, regardless of their class status. She explained some of the challenges of traveling outside her residential community. Not having a car can make traveling beyond the borders of one's neighborhood a challenge. It is a luxury to be able to come and go whenever one wants to and to have the financial means to purchase the nice things that are advertised on television or on billboards. This interview excerpt reveals that residents believe they deserve nice things, even if they cannot afford them, and the larger social order designates their race and class as justification for keeping such retail establishments out of their communities.

In Mara's account there is a distinction made between those who take the merchandise and those who purchase it. Mara explained that she didn't take the stolen merchandise as a means of implying that there is a difference between her and those who steal directly from stores. Yet only a few moments later, it seems that this statement was slightly reconsidered. She went on to say that those stealing and then reselling the merchandise "are just trying to live like the rest of us," which suggests that they are just trying to manage daily life in the inner city as she and others are. Mara pointed out that this exchange is reciprocal where "in a way we help each other out." This explains how each participant has a commodity, a service, or money that the other needs, and in turn they both help each other meet basic daily needs through this system of exchange, which occurs between members of a local social network. This community-based network complements that described by

Carol Stack, in which goods are most often bought and sold, rather than traded, among community members (1974, chap. 3). Nevertheless, these two methods of goods exchange share the central component of community. In the case Mara described, she considered herself supporting local underground entrepreneurs by purchasing the often stolen goods they have for sale. She also perceived these local hustlers as supporting the local community by acquiring and selling goods to residents that they wanted but could not otherwise access or afford. She described a type of mutual dependency between local residents who purchase goods and the hustlers who provide them. One party needs the goods, as is Mara's case, because she does not have a car and this restricts her access to mainstream retail businesses; on the occasions she can get to conventional retail stores she often cannot pay the prices these establishments charge for goods. In turn, the underground entrepreneurs need the revenue from the goods they sell out of their cars or homes to provide for their own basic needs. This system of exchange is mutually dependent on both parties remaining active participants in order for everyone to obtain the goods and money they need to keep their lives running from day to day.

Controlling Images

The importance of women in the inner city carefully crafting and recrafting their presentation of self is in large part a result of mainstream perceptions and portrayals of poor black womanhood. Patricia Hill Collins describes the powerful impact of dominant controlling images of black women as bad mothers, welfare queens, bitches, and whores and details how such labels have been deeply internalized by black and white men, women, and youth and thus quickly and routinely associated with black female bodies. Furthermore, such powerful images have become widely portrayed in the mainstream media, including music and television, and this has influenced the prevalent connection between these controlling labels and the image of the black woman in the minds of countless individuals all over the world (Collins 2005, chap. 4). Yet the power of such images and associations are further complicated by poverty and the day-to-day realities of living in suffering urban communities. For generations, the black poor have been labeled unrefined, loud, and uncivilized as a population and in terms of public behavior. Acceptance of such labels as true has encouraged a widely accepted distinction between the public behavior of poor urban blacks and the "conventional" middle class. In an effort to dispel the negative ideals and assessments associated with poor black womanhood, many women in the inner city creatively work to reinvent parts of their self-presentation. Keeping it fresh is a key component used to help buffer black women from the negative evaluations commonly made about them by outsiders.

In their landmark study of urban life, St. Clair Drake and Horace R. Cayton ([1945] 1993) note that the public behavior of poor blacks is expected to be loud, boisterous, and unrefined, the opposite of conventional middle-class American public behavior. Their description of this very particular kind of behavior reflects common assumptions about the self-presentation of poor inner-city blacks. This is where the "front" or presentation of self (Goffman 1959) is key. Those who are highly regarded socially, well educated, and refined take pride and value in how they present themselves and are received by the world. Drake and Cayton explain the significance of the well-manicured front as a symbol of progress—specifically for blacks living in urban areas that place clear limitations on upward mobility and on "getting ahead" socially and economically (Drake and Cayton [1945] 1993, 388–390, 519).

Elijah Anderson's study of young black men and public interactions describes the process of passing inspection as part of interacting in a street environment. He points out how multiple characteristics, including clothing, jewelry, race, gender, and age, work to mark someone as predator versus prey (Anderson 1990; see also Goffman 1971). Anderson underscores the efforts some young men take to offset and disprove many of the assumptions that outsiders have about urban neighborhoods. Many outsiders see these communities as breeding grounds for crime, danger, delinquency, drugs, prostitution, ignorance, and persistent poverty, and some residents attempt to refute the negative assumptions about the people who live in such communities through individual interactions. Keeping it fresh is a way of contradicting the controlling images of poor, black women; presenting a neat appearance enhanced by expensive clothes, shoes, and accessories also works as a type of campaign for respectability that connects these women to an aspect of a more respectable form of black femininity. Nevertheless, outsiders' destructive, oppressive, and controlling images of these women still persist.

WHAT IT MEANS TO "LOOK GOOD"

When discussing with respondents why keeping a fresh appearance is important, I repeatedly heard "I want others to see me differently"—specifically, as more than being poor. Keeping it fresh is an intentional aesthetic performance through which women use available material resources to challenge controlling images linked to being poor, female, and black, at least for a short time. This strategy helps these women to step away from the feelings of stigma or shame that come along with such labels. Alicia, a twenty-two-year-old black woman and longtime East Oakland resident, told me how her own experiences as a child informed how and why she wants her baby to always look fresh. "I like it when my baby has the newest clothes and shoes out of all the kids at her daycare," she explains. "I never had really nice stylish clothes when I was a kid, and I want my baby to have that. She needs to know that it is important to always look good. People see you different when you keep yourself up." Alicia shows that this project of "keeping yourself up" is fundamentally interactional. As she decides how to dress her baby she is processing past evaluations others have made about her self-presentation. She draws on her own experience of not having what she describes as fashionable clothing as a child. As a result, she feels that others perceive her differently, as *less than*. She has adopted this idea as a value of sorts in an effort to put off experiences of shame and discomfort for her own child. Alicia implies that others see a person as acceptable when they have a neat and fashionable appearance, a type of positive distinction. To be different in this case is to be seen as better than those deemed as disheveled or poorly presented. Many of the women I have talked to describe a disheveled appearance as "busted" or "janky"—that is, ugly, cheap, and of poor quality. In this case, *different* means presentable in a fashion acceptable by middle-class standards of appearance. Tiyanna, a twenty-four-year-old community resident, explained how she feels when she keeps it fresh through a system of sale and trade that operates within the local underground marketplace, particularly in light of how she struggles to make it every day while recognizing the legacy of struggle she fears she will pass on to her children: "I struggle every day of my life, and my two sons probably will too. It's cool having a nice outfit or some nice new shoes so you can at least look good while you out here fighting to try to make it." Tiyanna suggests the value in this presentation of self (Goffman 1959) while living a life complicated by continuous struggle and foreseeing this same existence for her children. It seems that keeping a clean, neat, and stylish appearance aids in managing this everyday fight. Engaging in this particular form of self-presentation operates as a display of confidence for Tiyanna as she manages her daily life. Looking good makes her feel better about herself and her children and how they cope with the struggles they encounter each day.

In her work on women and the politics of appearance, Wendy Chapkis emphasizes how a woman's appearance makes a statement about her race, class, gender, and sexuality—particularly in a social world divided by these categories. Physical appearance works to convey to onlookers whether one has a big paycheck or none at all or holds professional power or not. Such statements further indicate a person's belonging to a certain class, including all of the benefits or stigmas that accompany the determined status. Chapkis asserts that an evaluation of power is made based on visual statements of dress and demeanor (1986, 79–80). It is the outcome of such evaluations that women in poor urban communities hope to change through keeping it fresh. Kelly, a twenty-four-year-old lifelong East Oakland resident, told me why looking good is so important to her. "I have a lot to cry about," she explained. "I mean, my life has been hard for my age, but I still have to get up and go out and work and survive, and I want to try and feel good like everybody else, so I make it a point to look my best. It's important to me to stay fresh, and it feels good to stay fresh too. Who don't like it when their friends or somebody they know says, 'You look good' or 'That's a cute outfit'?"

Kelly explains how looking good is significant to her in the context of living a tough life. Being able to present herself in a way that makes her feel good despite having "a lot to cry about" exemplifies how keeping it fresh operates as a coping strategy, a method that women use to help manage the stress that accompanies troubled inner-city life. Though this strategy may not change public interactions for women like Kelly, it does make them feel good within the confines of their distressed urban lives, which even for a moment is a success.

In the following account Courtney, a twenty-five-year-old mother of two boys and one girl, describes how she feels when she can offer her children more than basic necessities and how she feels when she cannot:

> My kids are good. They listen and mind and don't start a lot of trouble at school. They are thankful for whatever I give them, but like a lot of kids they want new video games and jeans with glitter and brand-name this and brand-name that—stuff I can't afford. I feel bad, like I should be doing more as their mother when Christmas and birthdays come around and I can't give them something extra special. Last Christmas I was almost as excited as them when I bought a video game system they had been begging me for. It cost $300 on sale in the store and I got it for, like, $65 from one of these guys selling stuff near my house. It felt really good to see them so happy.

Women like Courtney mention feeling like "better women" (and specifically, "better mothers") when they are able to give their children things that they themselves never had as children but always wanted—popular toys, clothes, gym shoes, and the like. Yet these same women frequently describe their experiences of hostility and humiliation while shopping in local stores or just walking down the street. Many of them described how they didn't want to be seen as poor or treated as *less than*. Nevertheless, their treatment in public seemed to remain the same. Overall, my respondents did not report being treated with a great deal of kindness or respect when they dressed nicely, and they did not see their daily public interactions with others change to any degree that might be equivalent to how they perceived the nonpoor as being treated.

Keeping it fresh appears to operate largely as a coping strategy that helps these women manage the pressures of the stigmatized images of who they are. There are, however, consequences to keeping it fresh. It is about a feeling of distinguishing oneself from those considered less deserving of respect, and feeling good because one looks good in a place where there isn't a lot to feel good about. Although keeping it fresh does not transform the dominant controlling images of who black women are assumed to be and appear to be, this aesthetic performance is of value to these women as members of the community. To be recognized by others as respectable and to feel better about oneself because of such recognition even for a moment works to maintain a sense of personal dignity in a place that marks poor black women as unworthy.

Maintaining a fresh appearance for women in this urban space is a significant expression of normative notions of femininity, respectable blackness, and standardized conceptions of class. Alicia and Courtney (discussed earlier in the chapter) both told me that, as mothers, keeping a fresh appearance was about more than just them; it was about their children also. Courtney demonstrated gendered ideas about mothering as she described the positive feelings she experienced and how her role as a mother was in some ways reinforced when she could provide special gifts for her children—items that for her were usually unattainable outside the underground marketplace. Alicia viewed "looking good" as a value of sorts that she was already instilling in her infant daughter. These understandings of acceptable appearance and good mothering reflect a status other than that of the "bad black mother" (Collins 2005, 131), a status largely considered to be normative for poor inner-city black women. Alicia and Courtney keep it fresh in part to be recognized as respectable women and mothers. They present themselves and their children in a way that distances them from normative images of poverty and blackness. They purchase expensive clothes, shoes, and accessories for themselves and their children, a seemingly uncharacteristic behavior for women of their status. Both women demonstrate that for them looking good means adopting a style and quality of dress that signals middle-class notions of acceptable femininity and blackness. Even though both women are poor and black and live in the inner city, they work to display a particular image and to be recognized through their physical dress as other than poor, even to those in their neighborhood who know their true status. The fact that many residents in the neighborhood are familiar with the concept of keeping it fresh, and the impoverished status of others, keeps women like Alicia and Courtney from "passing" in their immediate community. Yet the work done to be *recognized* as someone more than poor remains central. To be recognized as respectable black women and mothers is a key motivation in using this strategy. In this way, these women accept normative models of white middle-class femininity and respectable blackness. To do this they contradict prevailing ideas about what it means to look like a poor black woman (Bettie 2003, 49–52; Collins 2005, chap. 4; Jones 2010, 7–12), which, in the words of one respondent, is "hair not done and garbage clothes, just ugly."

"I AM POOR, BUT I DON'T HAVE TO LOOK THAT WAY"

Many social workers, government officials, and members of the middle class have attacked poor blacks for using what limited resources they have to buy expensive goods when it appears that other needs are left unmet (Ladner 1971); if poor blacks would only realign their priorities and delay such pleasures, they would have a brighter future. Yet middle-class Americans, including the black middle class (many of whom live beyond their means), do not experience such stigma. Joyce A. Ladner emphasizes that for many young, poor, black girls who live without many of life's necessities, expensive and fashionable clothing can operate as a means of temporary compensation for so many of the things that they must go without. To be well dressed or better dressed in comparison to others locally can make one appear through her presentation of self to be equal or at times superior to peers and to those who subjugate her and her existence on a daily basis. Often, poor blacks are accused of being preoccupied with material goods, made evident by having expensive clothes while living in poverty. Yet the larger U.S. social order has proved to have a greater commitment to, and places a superior value on, goods and consumerism. This is apparent in the vastly uneven levels of resources allocated to social and human services versus those spent on war (Ladner 1971).

The role of luxury consumerism and the desire for such goods on the part of poor urban blacks and other groups in the United States is in large part a result of contemporary nationwide marketing strategies proving victorious (Nightingale 1995). Many poor blacks across gender lines embrace the American consumer culture in an effort to soothe the constant wounding of racial degradation and isolation and the distress of poverty. Yet stigma still persists for poor blacks when they are only embracing the American value of abundance as advertising strategies have intended. The accounts provided by women in this study reveal that due to the inadequate local retail sector, residents are often limited to purchasing necessary goods through the underground marketplace, the illicit system that provides a variety of often stolen products at prices well below retail and otherwise unavailable in the community.

Many of the women who live in East Oakland struggle to make ends meet, and traveling outside their community for goods and services takes extra time and money. Not only does buying and trading through the underground marketplace save these women time, but the goods for sale through this system come at a fraction of the manufacturer's suggested retail price, thus providing many residents the opportunity to acquire goods they otherwise could not afford. This makes the process of maintaining a stylish appearance enhanced by expensive clothes, shoes, and accessories possible. Even so, if there was a legitimate retail core in the neighborhood it is easy to imagine that residents like Mara would not be able to consistently afford the goods sold at retail prices; thus it is quite possible that many of these women would still engage in the underground marketplace as a means for keeping it fresh. Through maintaining this particular sort of appearance, poor inner-city residents have the chance to re-create their presentation of self, including the class status they present to others, though their true impoverished status remains the same. Although women are not actually changing their class position, they are using available resources to challenge common expectations that tend to complicate their encounters with others. Erica, a woman in her early twenties, described how she feels when she "looks" poor while out in public: "I can't stand it when people look at me and can say, 'She's poor.' Like they can just tell from how I look or how I dress. We were poor growing up, but my grandmother always did her best to have us looking good. Our clothes were always clean and ironed. I take pride in looking the best I can, and if buying my stuff off of the street is a part of it, then, oh well."

These comments explain how Erica feels when being subjected to the controlling image and label of poverty, and her experience gives a glimpse of some of the feelings that accompany negotiating her physical appearance as an identity marker that may reveal her class status. She talked about the immense pride she feels in looking her best and how the informal retail system in her community helps make this possible. Without this system in place she might not be able to present herself in this way, increasing the level of emotional labor and pain that can come with being—and appearing to be—poor. Brittney, a twenty-three-year-old East Oakland resident, described some of the complicated feelings she has around being marked as poor even when dressed nicely and the responses she receives from others when she keeps it fresh: "Sometimes people who I don't even know look at me like something is wrong when they see me dressed really nice. It's like I'm not supposed to have anything just because this is where I live."

Brittney's account describes the evaluation from others when a woman's physical dress defies prevailing images of what it looks like to be poor, and reveals how she interacts with the expectations of others—specifically, how she presents herself in a way that contradicts the expectations of others about how she should look because of where she lives. In this case the context of a poor urban neighborhood challenges the clean, neat, and expensive appearance Brittney presents. Through such an appearance she is working to explicitly defy dominant understandings of racialized poverty that are placed upon residents of inner-city communities. In addition to the categorical identities that mark her, like race and gender, it is also assumed that she is marked, and stigmatized, by racialized space.

Keeping It Fresh as a Gendered Strategy

Elaine Bell Kaplan notes that the harsh day-to-day realities of poor young black women include "[being] housed in threatening, drug-infested environments, schooled in jail-like institutions, and obstructed from achieving the American Dream." These women are stigmatized, "disqualified from full participation [in society] and . . . marked as deviant" (1997, xxi). These daily experiences encourage the development of strategies to manage survival within such troubled circumstances; such strategies are consistently critiqued by the young black women who employ them, and are constantly modified to fit the changing demands of daily life. The development and use of the creative survival strategies employed by black women in the inner city are an outcome of race, gender, and class inequalities rather than a unique characteristic of black culture (Kaplan 1997, 7).

Kaplan's findings align with Nikki Jones's discussion of situated survival strategies, and especially the ways in which women and girls present themselves in public and navigate urban space (i.e., situational avoidance; Jones 2010). As young women employ these strategies, they pay close attention to how they present themselves in public. In her work on young black mothers, Kaplan (1997) suggests that girls engage in three types of impression management: dressing up, avoidance, and revision. In the first instance, young women dress up—both in terms of their physical appearance and emotion. This tactic can work in two ways: as an emotionally protective mechanism and as a mask to hide certain stigmatized identity markers. Blackness and womanness are readily visible for most of these women, but the presentation of class is more malleable. If one can dress up and appear to transgress the boundary of poverty even within an impoverished community, the hope is to reduce class stigma, even if only in the short term. Robin D. G. Kelley (1993) discusses how dressing up operated for poor blacks in a historical context and describes how southern black sharecroppers, coal miners, tobacco farmers, and domestic workers used dressing up as a way of detaching from the humiliation of work. Kaplan (1997) states in her discussion of avoidance, the second type of impression management young women employ, that it involves maintaining the privacy of class status by staying away from institutions that could expose it (e.g., the welfare office). In the third form of impression management, revision, young women rewrite their personal story, omitting information that could expose their class status. The power to rewrite one's story allows for hope beyond current circumstance; the American dream remains within reach in a rewritten story.

In Erving Goffman's discussion of gender display, which can be understood as a form of "expressive behavior," he talks about the "controlling role of the performance" (1976, 1): how people providing a display can directly influence how they are perceived by viewers depending upon how they style themselves in terms of gender, hair, clothing, and the like, particularly over time. This is central to the work of keeping it fresh. Though it is not always assured, generally as a person's style and the interaction become routine, so does the perception of a particular identity that is being applied to them by a second party. Goffman shows that gender displays are a lot like any other type of ritualized forms of expression. Expressing one's class status through physical markers while interacting with others can mirror primary elements of the larger social structure and a person's place within it. Nevertheless, displays can just as easily refute the reality of the social situation or the status of the person providing them. Ultimately, displays give only a small indication of a much larger and complex social arrangement or identity (Goffman 1976).

Understanding gender as a role conceals the work required in producing gender in everyday encounters, while understanding gender as a display pushes it to the margin of interactions. Candace West and Don Zimmerman (1987) note how gender is an accomplishment that interactions are fundamentally organized around. They argue that members within an interaction organize their numerous and changing actions to express their gender category as it is understood within a given context. Understanding gender as an accomplishment requires understanding gender as an interaction that is evaluated by others with beliefs rooted in the biological differences in gender categories and gendered behavior.

Interactions are also organized around other categorical identities like race and class, and it is within social interaction that individuals represent themselves in connection to race, class, and gender. It is at this moment that other members of the interaction are summoned to evaluate those actions as suitable or not based on prevailing social understandings of natural and unnatural ways of being for members of the particular race, gender, and class category in question (West and

Fenstermaker 2002a, 142). The accomplishment of race, class, and gender through interactions works to either legitimate or refute existing social arrangements and expectations linked to particular groups (West and Fenstermaker 2002b, 53). For the women in this study, this means always being accountable to the expectations of what raced and gendered poverty looks like in their local community; each day when they leave their residences, they go on display for people they know and those they don't. The work of keeping it fresh is about contradicting the prevailing notions of what poverty looks like in terms of physical dress. This intentional form of self-presentation works to discredit any evaluation labeling those who keep it fresh as poor, if even for a moment. Women develop a presentation of style (marked by expensive clothes, shoes, and accessories) that they associate with normative expectations of what it means to look middle class to distinguish themselves as something better than poor. They present a version of self in this manner in an effort to be evaluated according to middle-class standards of dress and respectability. For those who know the truth and evaluate these women according to their lower-class status regardless of their self-presentation, the aim is to achieve a particular type of recognition, to be evaluated and recognized based on a higher standard of expectations than that commonly associated with poor black women in the inner city.

The particular ways in which women and girls present themselves in urban public space represent their efforts to distinguish themselves from "ghetto chicks," a derisive label for low-income women whose behavior, beliefs, and demeanor contrast with mainstream and black middle-class expectations of appropriate and respectable femininity (Jones 2010, 99; Thompson and Keith 2004, 58). Young women in the neighborhood want to be recognized as deserving respect based on their presentation of style. As they maintain a particular type of physical dress and presentation in interaction with others, they "do gender," "do race," and "do class" (West and Zimmerman 1987, 137), and they challenge the controlling images typically associated with poor black women and the dominant discourse in society—one that excludes the experiences of black women and girls.

The process of negotiating gender, race, and class through a particular style of self-presentation is complicated for women in the inner city. This process is about far more than just not fitting in or being perceived as more than poor. Craig Haney sheds light on the very specific experiences, influences, and impact of otherness within the larger context of systemic inequality; he discusses the presence of biographical racism and how it operates as the "accumulation of race-based obstacles, indignities, and criminogenic influences that characterize the life histories of so many African American capital defendants" (2005, 194). Haney explains that the "continued correlation of race with so many other painful and potentially damaging experiences in our society" directly shapes the life histories and biographies of those exposed to them (2005, 194). To further uncover some of the elements of biographical racism, he draws on urban poverty, the distress of chronic financial hardship, and the fact that African American youth are more likely to live under such conditions than are other youth. He notes the findings of several scholars and how many poor inner-city youth have discovered remarkable ingenuity in terms of developing coping strategies to manage their daily lives. Yet Haney reasserts Carl H. Nightingale's (1995) point that such learned expertise is "no match for the physical toll of poverty and its constant frustrations and humiliations" (Nightingale, quoted in Haney 2005, 195).

Haney notes other aspects of biographical racism that particularly impact large numbers of African American youth. These include encountering expressions of racial hatred, living in racially segregated neighborhoods, and enduring the suspicion that is widespread among persons in authority. Many black youth growing up in distressed inner-city communities also contend with violence in their neighborhoods and schools, and this puts them at further risk of victimization in places that should be physically and psychologically safe for them. Living under such circumstances informed by the long arm of biographical racism predisposes these youth for increased rates of posttraumatic stress disorder as well as troubled and problematic futures (Haney 2005, 195–197).

Through understanding some of the impact of biographical racism in addition to racialized poverty on the lives of poor black youth one may see how informal and illegal systems of retail sale and trade develop and operate in urban communities. In neighborhoods harshly affected by crime, joblessness, poverty, and a lack of local resources and retail establishments, developing independent retail sale and trade operations can be one of the few ways to supplement income for residents—including persons exiting the criminal justice system. Additionally, there is a demand for goods and institutions in such communities where residents are often confined; it is a market that many large and independent retail establishments choose not to enter.

The enormous force of biographical racism is illustrated not only through the lack of local resources, poverty, and social isolation present in communities like East Oakland but also through the emotional impact of stigma and inequality experienced by those who live there. For women like Mara, Alicia, and Kelly the strain of poverty is something they are all too familiar with. It is a painful reality many also see in their own children's future. A particularly distressing aspect of this experience of raced, classed, and gendered poverty is the side they must show the world each day through self-presentation. For women in the neighborhood, keeping it fresh operates as a buffer between themselves and public evaluations of who they are or are assumed to be—poor and unworthy of respect. While being recognized as respectable or passing as a member of the middle class is not guaranteed by keeping it fresh, performing this particular type of self-presentation works to distinguish these women from those seen as less worthy of respect. Being able to actively distinguish oneself from these further marginalized groups reinforces the notion that they are someone worthy of respect despite the prevailing notions and images that say otherwise. They are certain that no matter how they are perceived by neighbors, friends, or outsiders, they feel better when they look better, and this alone makes keeping it fresh important, particularly as they manage the daily struggles of distressed inner-city life.

What about the future of women who live in the inner city? Will they continue to feel the need to keep it fresh as a way to manage encounters complicated by their race, class, and gender? The current conditions of life in the troubled inner city assure that struggle is very likely to continue for its residents. The respondent accounts shared in this study suggest that the need to feel better about oneself while experiencing harsh living conditions, a lack of resources, and raced, classed, and gendered inequality is a reality for many women. Keeping it fresh is one way in which women work to perform a version of self they perceive as respectable in the hope of not only being treated with respect but also feeling better about themselves. Creative ways of negotiating local poverty and the ways in which residents go about trying to gain respect may change over time. In spite of this, the desire to be acknowledged as deserving of respect is sure to remain as long as prevailing notions continue to mark poor black women in urban settings as unworthy.

If more resources and legitimate businesses were to enter the community, the presence of poverty and systemic inequality would still persist, further complicating the lives of women who live there. The women who live in East Oakland under impoverished conditions and experience the stigma attached to living in poverty often envision much of their own struggle playing out in the lives of their children. As this tragic legacy is passed on, so must traditions of managing such lived realities. Keeping it fresh can operate as a tradition that children grow up with. It is a strategy that can be adjusted as necessary, but is fundamentally designed to help them use available material resources in such a way that challenges common expectations that complicate their encounters with others.

Conclusion

AJA IS THE thirty-one-year-old mother of seven-year-old Charles and two-year-old Callie. She describes Charles as a "really good kid" and adds, "He already earns good marks in school and his teacher always says how focused and well mannered he is." Aja expresses concern, however, for Charles's safety as he grows into a young African American man living in the inner city: "I am afraid that he could get killed out here for no reason. The police have already killed so many black kids, not to mention the violence from gangs and drug dealers too." In a society that marginalizes young black men, often labeling them as violent and criminal, Aja's concerns for Charles are common and regularly shared by other black mothers in the present study. Aja's great concern for the safety of her young daughter Callie is just as intense as her fear for Charles. She worries that

> the men she may get involved with [intimate partners] when she gets older, and just men on the street, will give her a hard time, not treating her with the respect that she deserves. When I think of Callie growing into a woman one day I am afraid of the pain and struggle that she is likely to face. I have experienced assaults both in and outside of the workplace on more occasions than I can count. While working at a fast-food restaurant I have had customers throw food at me, yell at me in an angry tone,

and call me out of my name [call me derogatory names]
just because. At home I have struggled with relationships,
including experiences with abuse. When I was four months
pregnant with Callie, her father and I were in a parking
lot arguing when he punched me in the face and I went
flying into the bushes. I have worked two jobs for most of
my adult life and participated in illegal work from time to
time just to make ends meet. This is a lot for anybody to
handle and I don't want that for my daughter, but I am
scared that it will happen anyway.

Aja's fear for the safety of her children reveals a troubling
reality for many poor inner-city black women as they work to
meet the demands of daily life under harsh conditions. Her
desire is for a safe and prosperous future for Charles and Callie,
yet she understands that struggles similar to those she has
experienced are likely to "happen anyway" for them. Aja's dis-
closure of the troubled and often humiliating interactions she
has had in the workplace, as well as violent encounters with
intimate partners, represents a knowledge of her own vulnerability as a poor black woman to distressed public interactions.
The experiences Aja describes also reveal the severity of the
struggle that she believes is likely to unfold in similar ways in
the lives of her children.

For many women living under similar conditions, such
a desire for safety and civility within social interactions is
common; for many residents of middle-class communities,
however, safe and civil public interaction is an expected component of daily life. The labor that is required of women like
Aja to negotiate and survive these encounters represents some
of the pain and struggle associated with "the grind" and routine
experiences with microinteractional assaults. In turn, the necessity of crafting and recrafting survival strategies and strategies
of resistance (such as interactional resistance and buffering) are

a central part of managing daily life in this setting. Aja's concern for the safety and future of her children uncovers the likeliness of these distressed interactions extending from one generation to the next.

In this study I have aimed to show how race, class, and gender are lived and negotiated each day through the routine public encounters experienced by black women like Aja and others living in the inner city. Through their day-to-day interactions we see a range of inequality and the way in which strategies for daily resistance to inequality unfold. The present study sheds light on the intense physical and emotional labor that women must do to meet the daily demands of life in a community often characterized by poverty and violence.

The interactions black women experience in poor inner-city neighborhoods uncover contemporary ideas about who they are and are not as poor black women. Respondent accounts disclose the power of creativity, the importance of community, and a will to carry on in the face of immense struggle. This is made evident through the innovative strategies women develop in an effort to survive when they could just give up. Daily encounters with public harassment, including sexual violence, have not deterred these women from working to provide for themselves and their families. Although routine troubled interactions complicate daily life in this distressed urban space, they haven't dismantled the community cohesion represented in local social support networks. Such commitments contradict prevailing ideas that outcomes of crime and violence can be the only result of poor urban communities.

The Future

The research herein reveals some key issues in the study of African American women and their experiences negotiating distressed urban life, yet raises some questions as well: What does the future look like for women who come of age in poor urban settings? Will the day-to-day experiences of these women continue to be shaped by troubled public encounters, including microinteractional assaults? As women struggle to provide for themselves and their families, will they need to work within the underground marketplace *and* maintain socially legitimate low-wage work in order to survive? This study underscores what is at stake for poor black women as they work to meet the demands of daily life under harsh conditions. Their vulnerability to public harassment and to acts or threats of sexual violence each time they ride the city bus, walk to work, buy groceries, or try to cash their paychecks is alarming. Still, these tasks must get done.

Current conditions assure that continued struggle is probable for both women and men in East Oakland. As I write this, we continue to experience an American crisis. Over the last several years we have witnessed the near disappearance of manufacturing jobs, financial disaster on Wall Street, an astounding number of home foreclosures, and enormous rates of unemployment. Such instability has increasingly impacted our poorest communities. We continue to see a steady decline in social services, public resources, and a steady growth in desperation within already underserved neighborhoods. These circumstances have reshaped the vulnerability and risk experienced by many as they negotiate the demands of daily life (Grusky, Western, and Wimer 2011).

As violence, poverty, and joblessness persist, so will the physical and emotional labor many women undertake to manage daily life in the inner city. It is critical, however, not to frame these women as problems based on the conditions they live in. Rather, it is significant to note that social problems such as violence and poverty shape not only the communities in which these women live but also many of their routine experiences. Yet amid the constant danger and stress associated with life in the inner city it is vital to explore the ways in which women negotiate daily life—and, ultimately, survival—within this environment. This book uncovers some of the everyday struggles black women face in this urban setting as well as the innovative strategies they develop in response to the troubled conditions around them (and which many were born into). This includes what women describe as "keeping it fresh" and the building and maintaining of social support networks designed to help sustain families. As women construct these ways of managing the distress around them they illustrate a kind of resiliency, commitment to community, and perseverance to get through another day.

In neighborhoods regularly exposed to violence, personal safety is a primary concern for many residents. For black women who are particularly vulnerable to street harassment, navigating public space can be especially challenging. Existing regulations designed to encourage community safety should encompass street harassment and microinteractional assaults as a problem. As illustrated in this study, such interactions are much more than routine interpersonal exchanges; they are hostile and potentially threatening encounters. Some residents endure these episodes day after day, and this restricts their local movement. Law enforcement does not have the trust of community members; several residents report police inactivity in the neighborhood regarding anything other than gun violence and "wish they would do more to keep us safe." It is necessary that all residents feel that their reports to police are taken seriously and attended to promptly; this kind of reliability can increase feelings of personal safety for residents and work to improve their confidence in police protection. Adjustment of current policies and the establishment of new forms of intervention designed to improve, regulate, and respond to instances of troubled public interactions in underserved communities are needed. Paying attention to the particular vulnerabilities residents face in the inner city is significant for implementing ways to better protect often ignored local populations.

In an effort to manage chronic poverty and underemployment, instituting programs that support the lives of residents
through job training and placement would positively impact
the East Oakland community. It is likely that residents would
be less inclined to turn to illegal jobs like those in the underground marketplace if they had local opportunities for job
training and guaranteed job placement. With a growth in the
legitimate workforce and a reduction in crime, the community
would likely become more attractive to major retailers, making
legitimate goods more affordable for residents. Additionally,
programs could encourage positive public interactions through
improving the living conditions of the previously unemployed
and reduce the constant stress associated with joblessness. This
microlevel progress would make living in communities shaped
by poverty and violence a bit easier to endure for the women
who must negotiate life in them each day.

APPENDIX

Field Research Methods in Urban Public Space

THE FINDINGS in this book are drawn from nearly two years of field research in an East Oakland neighborhood. During this time I conducted direct observation, participant observation, observant participation (Emerson, Fretz, and Shaw 1995) and in-depth interviews in East Oakland, an underprivileged community in an urban port city in northern California. I spent much of my youth in this neighborhood, and I was familiar with the layout of the community and some of the ongoing struggles here when I arrived to conduct field research.

Like many central city neighborhoods across the nation, this community has experienced the consequences of moving from a production-based to a service economy. Over the last thirty years the community has been shaped by underemployment, poverty, joblessness, and violence. In 2010, the city's total population was 390,724. Of the total population, nearly 30 percent (109,403) identified as black. Approximately 19.6 percent of all families and 20.8 percent of black families in Oakland lived below poverty. East Oakland is a predominantly black underserved inner-city neighborhood similar to central city neighborhoods in Baltimore, Chicago, Detroit, Philadelphia, and other cities (Anderson 1978, 1990, 1999; Liebow 1967; Whyte 1993; Wilson 1980, 1987, 1996). These factors make it an ideal setting in which to observe the complexities of living in distressed urban space while also examining the realities of how

U.S. Census Bureau, Census Tract Data, Oakland, California

People	Oakland	California
Population, 2010	390,724	37,253,956
Persons under 5 years, percent, 2010	6.7%	6.8%
Persons under 18 years, percent, 2010	21.3%	25.0%
Persons 65 years and over, percent, 2010	11.1%	11.4%
Female persons, percent, 2012	51.5%	50.3%
White persons, percent, 2010	34.5%	57.6%
Black persons, percent, 2010	28%	6.2%
American Indian and Alaska Native persons, percent, 2010	0.8%	1.0%
Asian persons, percent, 2010	16.8%	13.0%
Native Hawaiian and other Pacific Islander persons, percent, 2010	0.6%	0.4%
Persons of Hispanic or Latino origin, percent, 2010	25.4%	40.1%
Education and Work		
High school graduate or higher, percent age 25+, 2007–2011	79.5%	80.8%
Bachelor's degree or higher, percent age 25+, 2007–2011	37.2%	30.2%
Veterans, 2007–2011	16,734	1,997,566
Housing and Income		
Living in same house one year or longer, percent, 2007–2011	83.4%	84.2%
Housing units, 2010	169,710	13,680,081
Housing units in multiunit structures, percent, 2007–2011	51.9%	30.8%
Households, 2007–2011	154,537	12,433,172
Persons per household, 2007–2011	2.48	2.91
Per capita income, 2011	$31,675	$29,634
Median household income, 2007–2011	$51,14	$61,632
Persons below poverty level, percent, 2007–2011	19.6%	14.4%
Geography		
Land area in square miles, 2010	55.79	155,779.22
Persons per square mile, 2010	7,004.0	239.1

Source: U.S. Census Bureau, "QuickFacts: Oakland city, California." Accessed January 26, 2012. http://quickfacts.census.gov/qfd/states/06000.html

poor black women and girls develop and define their day-to-day survival strategies.

I took up residence in this community during the length of my study. Four to five days per week for two to five hours per day I systematically observed the daily routines of residents. Many of my observations emerged from the time I spent in and around Check-N-Pay, a neighborhood check-cashing establishment; Frank's Liquor, a popular liquor store in the neighborhood; and Star Market, a local grocery store. These businesses are three of the central commercial organizations in the vicinity. Several other storefront businesses were vacant or in business for short periods during much of the time I was carrying out this study. Having lived in this neighborhood some years prior to beginning this research, I knew that each of these establishments had remained open and active over the past several years and had outlasted much of the other commercial activity in the neighborhood.

I had easy access to the three businesses; each was a short distance from where I lived in the neighborhood. I gained entrée at Frank's Liquor and Star Market as a regular patron, and as such I was able to observe the interactions between other regular and infrequent customers and store personnel in a discreet way. As a customer I was also able to routinely experience my own interactions within these businesses.

I sought out services at Check-N-Pay infrequently. I spent much of my time observing from the back of the store near a large bulletin board where local announcements were posted. As I stood in the rear of the store, which was often filled with customers, it was easy for me to blend into the crowd as I observed the interactions around me. From this location I had a full view of the front of the business where customers were conducting transactions. I would take down and throw away old flyers posted on the bulletin board or on the wall about once a week, which would usually earn me a thank-you shouted from a store employee shielded behind the plexiglass wall that separates staff from customers. This "favor" of managing the bulletin board area usually kept me from being aggressively thrown out of Check-N-Pay for not cashing a check or purchasing another service while in the establishment.[1]

I became a fixture outside these businesses also, observing nearby bus stops and sidewalks. I saw who came and went and what kinds of interactions they had on the street in the neighborhood. Being outside allowed me a usually uninterrupted view of patrons as they entered and exited the businesses and offered me a chance to see several interactions that became aggressive, where customers were forced outside the buildings and armed store security guards became involved. Additionally, I routinely engaged in informal interviews and conversations with local customers as they came and went from these businesses or loitered around the area. I also talked with other neighborhood residents who passed by regularly. These exchanges were with both men and women; the majority identified as black, and they ranged in age from early adulthood through middle age.[2]

While observing in and around Check-N-Pay, Frank's Liquor Store, Star Market, and on the street in the neighborhood, I carried a small notebook with me to record jottings.[3] In an effort to collect and record descriptive accounts and encounters while in the field I developed my jottings into field notes as soon as possible after leaving the field sites each day. I later typed a more polished, extended version of my field notes, which I kept password protected on my computer. I separated my observations into categories including reflections, dialogue, details of encounters, and preliminary analysis (Emerson et al. 1995).

After spending a significant amount of time in these settings, and after having developed a friendly relationship with some of the people who lived in the neighborhood, I began to conduct formal, semistructured interviews with women I saw on repeated occasions. I chose to conduct interviews to further explore themes that first emerged during my observations. The interviews enhanced my data set with firsthand accounts of the types of experiences women have in this setting from day to day.

I selected my formal interviewees based on their gender, age, race, and residential location. Each interviewee had to identify as female, be over the age of eighteen, identify as black or African American, and live in or immediately around East Oakland. After completing an interview, I asked respondents if they knew of others who might be interested in talking to me. These referrals made it possible for me to carry out sixteen formal semistructured interviews and eleven follow-up interviews with black women who were local residents. Each woman had lived in the neighborhood a minimum of seven years, with the majority living there most of their lives.

I conducted interviews in several locations, including bus stops (three interviews), a coffee shop (one interview), fast-food restaurants (two interviews), and outside a local community center (four interviews) as well as over the telephone (six interviews). I noticed some key differences in the data I collected depending upon where the interview was conducted. The interviews held on the street, such as at bus stops or outside the local community center, seemed to trigger particularly vivid descriptions of troubled interactions and experiences had by the women. In most cases they described encounters of violence or harassment that occurred in close proximity to or in similar surroundings to where we stood. On several occasions women would repeatedly point to the ground on which we stood or to a nearby business or building to emphasize that this is where the disturbing scene they were reliving for me had originally taken place. I noticed a similar pattern when carrying out interviews at a local fast-food restaurant. This

Formal Interviews

Pseudonym	Age	Race	Gender	Years lived in East Oakland	Number of children
Amber*	19	Black	F	19	(Pregnant, first child)
Angel	18	Black	F	18	0
Courtney*	25	Black	F	25	3
Kira*	19	Black	F	9	1
Lauren*	22	Black	F	22	1
Leslie	23	Black	F	23	1
Mara*	23	Black	F	23	1
Mecca*	23	Black	F	18	2
Michelle*	19	Black	F	19	1
Myisha*	24	Black	F	24	0
Nicole	21	Black	F	21	1
Ruth*	19	Black	F	9	1
Shante*	22	Black	F	15	0
Terri*	21	Black	F	9	0
Tiyanna	24	Black	F	24	2
Vanessa	24	Black	F	24	2

Note: *Participated in follow-up interviews.

restaurant, which was familiar to the women I interviewed, served as a reminder of previous encounters on or around its premises. For example, when talking to a woman about an altercation she had been involved in at the local grocery store just days earlier, the conversation began to shift to a description of an aggressive encounter she once had in the parking lot of the fast-food restaurant where we sat.

When conducting telephone interviews I was initially concerned about not being able to see the respondents and their body language and gestures. I felt this could hinder how the interview progressed. But I found that the familiarity

Informal Interviews and Conversations

Pseudonym	Age	Race	Gender	Years lived in East Oakland	Number of children
Aja	31	Black	F	31	2
Alicia	22	Black	F	14	1
Amaya	20	Black	F	12	0
Avis	50	Black	F	50	4
Brittney	23	Black	F	12	2
Charles	51	Black	M	42	5
Erica	21	Black	F	21	0
Jennifer	24	Black	F	24	2
Kelly	24	Black	F	24	(Pregnant, first child)
Monique	24	Black	F	24	0
Ms. Jenny	53	Black	F	48	4
Ms. Loretta	58	Black	F	57	6
Ms. Thomas	54	Black	F	54	3
Ms. Virginia	76	Black	F	62	1
Rachel	21	Black	F	21	(Guardian of 1)
Robert	42	Black	M	42	(Guardian of 2)
Ron	48	Black	M	35	2
Shameeah	19	Black	F	19	0
Tanya	39	Black	F	17	1
Tiffany	26	Black	F	26	3

established through talking informally with participants on several occasions before the formal interview worked to ease the interaction some. Julie Bettie describes how girls' one-on-one telephone conversations about what is happening in their lives are commonplace for many. As a result the telephone can be a comfortable place for them to share their daily experiences and also a key site for ethnographers (2003, 28–30). I noticed that several women would begin answering one of my questions over the telephone by drawing on experiences and interactions we had discussed briefly in person on earlier occasions, yet now they spoke in more detail. Referencing our earlier discussions during the formal interview was one way that some women seemed to increase their comfort within this one-on-one, but not face-to-face, conversation.

I relied on a set of written questions as a framework for the interviews but let participants share as much information as they felt comfortable. I began each interview by collecting demographic information, including the participant's age, race, gender, the number of years she had lived in East Oakland, if she was a parent, and—if so—the number of children she had. I opened each interview by asking the respondent to describe the neighborhood for me. I then used the following guiding questions to frame the interviews:

- How do you get along with your neighbors and other residents?
- Have you had any experiences with strangers or people you don't know in this community?
- Have you ever had any unwanted interactions with people you don't know in the neighborhood?
- How do you describe the experience of black women here?
- What type of work do you do to make money?
- Where do you usually buy clothes and goods for yourself and your family?
- Have you or anyone you know ever purchased clothes, shoes, or other goods from somewhere other than a store or business?
- What comes to mind when you think of violence in the neighborhood?
- Is survival a serious concern for people in the neighborhood?

These guiding questions and more helped to draw out vivid descriptions of interpersonal violence, harassment, feelings of invisibility, poverty, how living in this space feels, and what strategies are used to stay safe as well as manage the discomfort of living in this distressed urban community.

Each interview was digitally recorded, and at the end of each conversation I took jottings on the interview. Interviews lasted between twenty and forty-five minutes. As with my field notes, upon leaving each interview I transcribed the conversation and developed my jottings into full descriptive notes as soon as possible. After conducting initial interviews I held several follow-up conversations with eleven of my original interviewees. As a part of the follow-up conversations I shared some of the observations recorded in my field notes with my participants. I sought out their opinions regarding how I was interpreting the neighborhood versus their own perspectives on it. Sharing data with local residents and receiving or not receiving their validation (Burgess 1984) helped me to further examine and remain conscious of how my experiences and interpretations differed from theirs.

Upon completing data collection I began open coding my data with a detailed line-by-line read of the material (Emerson et al. 1995). As a part of my data coding process I utilized a qualitative software analysis application as a tool to help organize my data. This data management system is designed to help systematize mixed method research data. Once open coding was complete, I conducted a more focused coding process with a second read of the material to begin a detailed analysis of the notes and interviews. At this stage I connected themes in the data that I had not immediately seen on the initial review and extracted and further developed key themes through integrative memos.[4]

Throughout my research process I exercised inductive reasoning. Beyond my determined research questions I did not apply any prearranged hypotheses or categories to this study. This was helpful in managing the challenge of bias in the research (Emerson et al. 1995). This method allowed me to add and take away from my questions and gave me the opportunity to produce insights about my sample population and setting more freely as themes developed. The ethnographic discoveries of "grinding," microinteractional assaults, and "keeping it fresh" were all developed using this inductive process.

Qualitative methods are useful in exploring how black women experience interactions in an urban community. Ethnographic methods are a valuable way to get at answering questions about how individuals produce meaning through social interaction. Ethnography also emphasizes the social context and setting in which such meanings are produced (Strauss 1987). In this study I have triangulated data collected using participant observation, direct observation, and interviews in an effort to capture the most complete representation of experiences shared by black women in East Oakland. Being there allowed me to see for myself how these interactions unfolded, while interviews helped me to better understand how women describe and evaluate these interactions for themselves. There are challenges that come along with qualitative research methods. How I observed, interpreted, and reported my research findings was shaped by my own categorical identities and personal experiences, as is the case with all ethnographers. In addition, because I was limited to one research site and to the participants at that site I cannot make strong claims about the generalizability of my findings, although it is likely that women who live under similar conditions will find some similarities in the experiences reported on here.

ACKNOWLEDGMENTS

IN MANY WAYS this book began long before my formal training as an ethnographer. Growing up in East Oakland, I spent years walking the streets of the community as I traveled to and from school, work, the grocery store, and so on. It was then that I first became troubled by the routine public interactions and encounters black women and girls faced, with violence, hostility, harassment, and humiliation being a part of each day. Returning as a graduate student I employed my ethnographic training in a quest to uncover what exactly women here were encountering, what their interactions mean, and how they make sense of these daily lived experiences. I was disturbed by the trauma that resulted from such encounters and equally intrigued by the conditions under which these realities were unfolding. *The Grind* is an ethnographic account of how black women and girls work tirelessly to navigate poor inner-city life and the myriad ways in which it is complicated by their race and gender. To the women who allowed me into their community and their lives, thank you for sharing your important stories.

Over the last several years, many people have graciously offered their insight, encouragement, wisdom, and support to help bring this book to fruition. I am so very grateful and would like to acknowledge them here; please forgive any inadvertent omissions.

As a graduate student in the Department of Sociology at the University of California–Santa Barbara (UCSB) I received tremendous support, mentoring, and a deep commitment to this project from Nikki Jones, Sarah Fenstermaker, and George Lipsitz. Their encouragement, criticism, and counsel have helped me stretch and grow as both a scholar and a human being. I am forever thankful to Nikki Jones for her consistent and careful reading, thoughtful recommendations, and ongoing mentorship; her dedication to improving the lives of black women and girls has been a critical force throughout this project, and I hope her influence and guidance is clear in this book. Sarah Fenstermaker challenged me to be sharper and more critical in my assertions and gave me the confidence to wrestle with my arguments to push them further; I thank her for her ongoing inspiration, mentorship, and generosity. George Lipsitz has influenced me beyond words; his unfaltering support throughout my journey has seen me through some of my toughest days and greatest victories as a scholar. His dedication to scholarship, activism, and to human kind is exemplary, and his work and wisdom continue to shape my scholarship and teaching. I am grateful to G. Reginald Daniel, who has provided guidance, inspiration, and friendship during my time at UCSB and beyond.

This research also benefited from the financial support of several fellowships at various stages of my career, including the National Science Foundation–University of California Diversity Initiative for Graduate Study in the Social Sciences Summer Research Fellowship; the William T. Grant Foundation Mentor Supplement Award (with Nikki Jones); the UCSB Disabled Students Program; Ridley-Tree Scholarship; the UCSB Graduate Division Dissertation Fellowship; and the Research, Scholarly, and Creative Activity Award from California State University, Dominguez Hills (CSUDH).

I am deeply grateful to my colleagues and students at CSUDH for all that they continue to teach me; It is a privilege and a joy to work and learn with you. I am thankful to the

Dean's Office in the College of Natural and Behavioral Sciences at CSUDH and to Kara Dellacioppa, chair of the Department of Sociology, for providing the resources necessary for completing this manuscript. I am especially grateful to the Department of Sociology for providing an enthusiastic and encouraging space in which to complete this book. Thank you to my colleagues Katy M. Pinto, La Tanya Skiffer, José Prado, Joanna Perez, Kelin Li, Matthew Mutchler, Gretel Vera-Rosas, Jeb Middlebrook, Sohaila Shakib, and Raman Brar. I am forever grateful to the members of the Warriors' Writing Group for their ongoing support, wisdom, encouragement, and optimism; the shared commitment to the fight for justice and equality is exceptional, and their intellectual stimulation and friendship is a reminder of the joy that can come within the struggle for justice. I also extend my appreciation and thanks to Keisha Paxton and the CSUDH Faculty Development Center for resources that helped support my work on this project.

I am grateful to the many colleagues and friends (some of whom are already mentioned above) who have supported me and this work in a variety of forms, including reading this work in varying stages and offering immeasurable feedback, thoughtful insight, enthusiasm, and encouragement. Thank you also to Christopher Bickel, Kenly Brown, Joan Budesa, Jordan T. Camp, James Cantres, Tomás Carrasco, Carla Coco-Boutté, Alison Dahl Crossley, Janette Diaz, FC, Kelly Foster, Jerry Flores, Bridget Harr, Christina Jackson, Tonya Lindsey, Monica Lomeli, Patrick Lopez-Aguado, Veronica Montes, Daniel Olmos, Steven Osuna, Nathalie Pierre, Carolyn Pinedo-Turnofsky, Jennifer Rogers-Brown, Rebecca Romo, Xuan Santos, Denise Segura, Barbara Tomlinson, Angel Valdivia, and the late Clyde Woods.

I thank Debra Guckenheimer, Hillary Potter, and the anonymous reviewers of the manuscript for their critical suggestions and support of this project. I am grateful to my editor, Peter Mickulas, for his enthusiasm and commitment to this project. The outstanding editorial work of Sean Mannion improved this manuscript enormously.

Finally, I am very fortunate to be surrounded by an amazing group of family and friends. To my grandparents, aunts, uncles, cousins, siblings, and friends outside of academia, thank you for your love and for being by my side every step of the way. I owe tremendous gratitude to my father, Robert L. McCurn, for always pushing me to be my best; his wisdom, work ethic, and love continue to have an impact on me, more than he'll ever know. To my mother, Sharon C. McCurn, who was my very first teacher and has always been my greatest supporter, words cannot adequately describe your contribution to this book; you have shared my joys and struggles, offered compassion and critique, and never once wavered in your commitment and faith in me and this work. To you I dedicate this book.

Notes

Introduction

1. The names of participants, businesses, and neighborhoods are pseudonyms.
2. Since the early 2000s the city's redevelopment agency and mayor's office has worked to revitalize commercial retail space and develop housing units in downtown Oakland. Only since about 2005 has the area begun to grow with the addition of downtown area neighborhoods such as The Uptown, a district that houses many new retail businesses, restaurants, entertainment venues, and recently constructed housing units.

Chapter 1   "Grinding": Living and Working in East Oakland

1. Amber's description of the measures she takes to stay safe in her neighborhood is similar to the case of "Danielle" described in Jones 2010, 67–68. These cases show how women and girls living under similar conditions are likely to make similar choices.

Chapter 2   "It Happens All the Time": Day-to-Day Experiences with Microinteractional Assaults

Earlier versions of this analysis appear in Jones and McCurn 2015 and McCurn 2017.

1. For further discussion of horizontal violence, "violence expressed toward members of the same group or other oppressed groups," see Irwin and Chesney-Lind 2008, 843.
2. For further incidents of racial discrimination while shopping, see Williams 1991, 44–47.

CHAPTER 3 "I AM NOT A PROSTITUTE": HOW YOUNG
BLACK WOMEN CHALLENGE SEXUAL HARASSMENT ON
THE STREET

1. Miller notes that "recent research has found that—in addition to
   other forms of violence—violence against women is also heightened in disadvantaged communities" (2008, 40).

APPENDIX

1. For further discussion of taking on a role in a setting, see Emerson,
   Fretz, and Shaw (1995), chap. 1.
2. My own categorical identities were likely significant in the
   research process and had an impact on my understanding, the
   development of theory, and the overall analysis of this work.
3. Emerson et al. (1995) describe "jottings" as short written notes
   designed to trigger the field researcher's memory about key
   interactions, observations, and events taking place in the field.
   These jottings are to help the researcher more thoroughly recall
   detailed descriptions of the setting when writing full field notes.
4. Through integrative memos the ethnographer begins to identify
   and link themes found in their coded field notes (Emerson et al.,
   1995).

References

Anderson, Elijah. 1978. *A Place on the Corner.* Chicago: University of Chicago Press.
———. 1990. *Streetwise: Race, Class, and Change in an Urban Community.* Chicago: University of Chicago Press.
———. 1999. *Code of the Street: Decency, Violence, and the Moral Life of the Inner City.* New York: Norton.
———. 2011. *Cosmopolitan Canopy: Race and Civility in Everyday Life.* New York: Norton.
Bettie, Julie. 2003. *Women without Class: Girls, Race, and Identity.* Berkeley: University of California Press.
Bohn, Sarah. 2011. "Poverty in California." Public Policy Institute of California. Accessed September 25, 2012. http://www.ppic.org/main /publication_show.asp?i=261.
Burgess, Robert G. 1984. *In the Field.* London: Allen and Unwin.
Callahan, Sara B. Dykins. 2008. "Academic Outings." *Symbolic Interaction* 31(4): 351–375.
Caskey, John P. 1994. *Fringe Banking: Check-Cashing Outlets, Pawnshops, and the Poor.* New York: Russell Sage Foundation.
Chapkis, Wendy. 1986. *Beauty Secrets: Women and the Politics of Appearance.* Boston: South End.
Chesney-Lind, Meda, and Lisa Pasko. 2004. *The Female Offender: Girls, Women, and Crime.* Thousand Oaks, CA: Sage.
Collins, Patricia Hill. 1986. "The Emerging Theory and Pedagogy of Black Women's Studies." *Feminist Issues* 6(1): 3–17.
———. 2000. *Black Feminist Thought: Knowledge, Consciousness, and the Politics of Empowerment.* New York: Routledge.
———. 2005. *Black Sexual Politics: African Americans, Gender, and the New Racism.* New York: Routledge.
Costa Vargas, João H. 2006. *Catching Hell in the City of Angeles: Life and Meaning of Blackness in South Central Los Angeles.* Minneapolis: University of Minnesota Press.
Davis, Deirdre. 1994. "The Harm That Has No Name: Street Harassment, Embodiment, and African American Women." *UCLA Women's Law Journal* 4(2): 133–178.
DeVault, Marjorie L. 1994. *Feeding the Family: The Social Organization of Caring as Gendered Work.* Chicago: University of Chicago Press.

Drake, St. Claire, and Horace R. Cayton. (1945) 1993. *Black Metropolis: A Study of Negro Life in a Northern City*. Reprint, Chicago: University of Chicago Press.

Edgerton, Robert B. 1993. *The Cloak of Competence*. Berkeley: University of California Press.

Emerson, Robert M., Rachel I. Fretz, and Linda Shaw. 1995. *Writing Ethnographic Fieldnotes*. Chicago: University of Chicago Press.

Feagin, Joe R., and Karyn D. McKinney. 2003. *The Many Costs of Racism*. Lanham, MD: Rowman and Littlefield.

Feagin, Joe R., and Melvin P. Sikes. 1994. *Living with Racism: The Black Middle-Class Experience*. Boston: Beacon.

Fee, Elizabeth, and Nancy Krieger. 1994. *Women's Health, Politics and Power: Essays on Sex/Gender, Medicine, and Public Health*. Amityville, NY: Baywood.

Fenstermaker, Sarah, and Candace West. 2002. *Doing Gender, Doing Difference: Power, Inequality, and Institutional Change*. New York: Routledge.

Gaines, Kevin. 1996. *Uplifting the Race: Black Leadership, Politics, and Culture in the Twentieth Century*. Chapel Hill: University of North Carolina Press.

Gardener, Carol Brooks. 1980. "Passing By: Street Remarks, Address Rights, and the Urban Female." *Sociological Inquiry* 50(3–4): 328–356.

———. 1995. *Passing By: Gender and Public Harassment*. Berkeley: University of California Press.

Garfinkel, Harold. 1956. "Conditions of Successful Degradation Ceremonies." *American Journal of Sociology* 61(5): 420–424.

Goffman, Erving. 1959. *The Presentation of Self in Everyday Life*. New York: Doubleday.

———. 1963. *Behavior in Public Places: Notes on the Social Organization of Gatherings*. New York: Free Press of Glencoe.

———. 1971. *Relations in Public: Microstudies of the Public Order*. New York: Basic Books.

———. 1976. "Gender Display." *Studies in the Anthropology of Visual Communication* 3(2): 69–77.

Gregory, Stephen. 1998. *Black Corona: Race and the Politics of Place in an Urban Community*. Princeton, NJ: Princeton University Press.

Grusky, David B., Bruce Western, and Christopher Wimer. 2011. *The Great Recession*. New York: Russell Sage Foundation.

Haney, Craig. 2005. *Death by Design: Capital Punishment as a Social Psychological System*. New York: Oxford University Press.

Higginbotham, Evelyn Brooks. 1994. *Righteous Discontent: The Women's Movement in the Black Baptist Church, 1880–1920*. Cambridge, MA: Harvard University Press.

Hinton, Eric L. 2003. "Microinequities: When Small Slights Lead to Huge Problems in the Workplace." *DiversityInc*. Accessed December 21, 2011. http://www.michelemmartin.com/files/small-slights-and-huge-problems.pdf

Hollander, Jocelyn A. 2001. "Vulnerability and Dangerousness: The Construction of Gender through Conversation about Violence." *Gender and Society* 15(1): 83–109.

———. 2009. "The Roots of Resistance to Women's Self-Defense." *Violence against Women* 15(5): 574–594.

Hollander, Jocelyn A., and Rachel L. Einwohner. 2004. "Conceptualizing Resistance." *Sociological Forum* 19(4): 533–554.

Hughes, Everett C. 1945. "Dilemmas and Contradictions of Status." *American Journal of Sociology* 50(5): 353–359.

———. 1994. *On Work, Race, and the Sociological Imagination*. Chicago: University of Chicago Press.

Irwin, Katherine, and Meda Chesney-Lind. 2008. "Girls' Violence: Beyond Dangerous Masculinity." *Sociology Compass* 2(3): 837–855.

Jenness, Valerie, and Sarah Fenstermaker. 2014. "Agnes Goes to Prison: Gender among Transgender Inmates in Prisons for Men and the Pursuit of the 'Real Deal.'" *Gender and Society* 28(1): 5–31.

Jones, Nikki. 2008. "Working 'the Code': On Girls, Gender, and Inner-City Violence." *Australian and New Zealand Journal of Criminology* 41(1): 63–83.

———. 2010. *Between Good and Ghetto: African American Girls and Inner-City Violence*. New Brunswick, NJ: Rutgers University Press.

Jones, Nikki, and Alexis McCurn. 2015. "Black Girls, Gender, and Violence." In *Understanding Diversity*, edited by C. M. Renzetti and R. M. Kennedy-Bergen, 78–91. New York: Pearson.

Kaplan, Elaine Bell. 1997. *Not Our Kind of Girl: Unraveling the Myths of Black Teenage Motherhood*. Berkeley: University of California Press.

Kelley, Robin D. G. 1994. *Race Rebels: Culture, Politics, and the Black Working Class*. New York: Free Press.

Kissling, Elizabeth Arveda. 1991. "Street Harassment: The Language of Sexual Terrorism." *Discourse Society* 2(4): 451–460.

Krieger, Nancy. 1990. "Racial and Gender Discrimination: Risk Factors for High Blood Pressure?" *Social Science and Medicine* 30(12): 1273–1281.

Ladner, Joyce A. 1971. *Tomorrow's Tomorrow: The Black Woman*. Garden City, NY: Doubleday.

Leadbeater, Bonnie J., and Niobe Way. 1996. *Urban Girls: Resisting Stereotypes and Creating Identities*. New York: New York University Press.

Liebow, Elliott. 1967. *Tally's Corner: A Study of Negro Streetcorner Men*. Boston: Little, Brown.

Logan, Laura S. 2011. "The Case of the Killer Lesbians." The Public Intellectual. Accessed January 31, 2012. http://thepublicintellectual.org/2011/07/18/the-case-of-the-killer-lesbians/.

Massey, Douglas S. 2007. *Categorically Unequal: The American Stratification System*. New York: Russell Sage Foundation.

Massey, Douglas S., and Nancy A. Denton. 1993. *American Apartheid: Segregation and the Making of the Underclass.* Cambridge, MA: Harvard University Press.

McCurn, Alexis S. 2017. "'I Am Not a Prostitute': How Young Black Women Challenge Sexual Harassment on the Street." *Sociological Focus* 50(1): 52–65.

McCurn, Alexis S. 2018. "'Keeping It Fresh': How Young Black Women Negotiate Self-Representation and Controlling Images in Urban Space." *City & Community* (forthcoming).

McKinsey Global Institute. 2009. "Analysis of Consumer Spending and U.S. Economic Growth from 2000–2007." Accessed October 11, 2011. http://www.mckinsey.com/insights/mgi/research/financial_markets.

Miller, Jody. 2008. *Getting Played: African American Girls, Urban Inequality, and Gendered Violence.* New York: New York University Press.

Nielsen, Laura Beth. 2004. *License to Harass: Law, Hierarchy, and Offensive Public Speech.* Princeton, N.J.: Princeton University Press.

Nightingale, Carl H. 1995. *On the Edge: A History of Poor Black Children and Their American Dreams.* New York: Basic Books.

Olesen, Virginia. 2005. "Early Millennial Feminist Qualitative Research." In *The Sage Handbook of Qualitative Research*, edited by Denzin Lincoln, 235–278. Thousand Oaks, CA: Sage.

Pattillo, Mary. 2008. *Black on the Block: The Politics of Race and Class in the City.* Chicago: University of Chicago Press.

Pierce, Chester M., Jean V. Carew, Diane Pierce-Gonzalez, and Deborah Willis. 1978. "An Experiment in Racism: TV Commercials." In *Television and Education*, edited by C. M. Pierce, 62–88. Beverly Hills, CA: Sage.

Rank, Mark Robert. 1994. *Living on the Edge: The Realities of Welfare in America.* New York: Columbia University Press.

Rhomberg, Chris. 2004. *No There There: Race, Class, and Political Economy in Oakland.* Berkeley: University of California Press.

Roschelle, Anne R. 1997. *No More Kin: Exploring Race, Class, and Gender in Family Networks.* Thousand Oaks, CA: Sage.

Sampson, Robert J., Steven W. Raudenbush, and Felton Earls. 1998. *Neighborhood Collective Efficacy—Does It Help Reduce Violence?* Washington, DC: National Institute of Justice.

Scott, Lionel D. 2003. "The Relation of Racial Identity and Racial Socialization to Coping with Discrimination among African American Adolescents." *Journal of Black Studies* 33(4): 520–538.

Segura, Denise A. 1984. "Chicanas and Triple Oppression in the Labor Force." In *Chicana Voices: Intersections of Class, Race, and Gender*, edited by Teresa Córdova, Norma Cantú, Gilberto Cardenas, Juan García, and Christine M. Sierra, 47–65. Austin, TX: Center for Mexican American Studies.

Self, Robert O. 2003. *American Babylon: Race and the Struggle for Postwar Oakland.* Princeton, NJ: Princeton University Press.

Sharkey, Patrick, and Felix Elwert. 2011. "The Legacy of Disadvantage: Multigenerational Neighborhood Effects on Cognitive Ability." *American Journal of Sociology* 116(6): 1934–1981.

Sheffield, Carole J. 1987. "Sexual Terrorism: The Social Control of Women." In *Analyzing Gender: A Handbook of Social Science Research*, edited by Beth B. Hess and Myra Marx Ferree, 171–189. Thousand Oaks, CA: Sage.

Small, Mario Luis. 2004. *Villa Victoria: The Transformation of Social Capital in a Boston Barrio.* Chicago: University of Chicago Press.

Solorzano, Daniel, Miguel Ceja, and Tara Yosso. 2000. "Critical Race Theory, Racial Microaggressions, and Campus Racial Climate: The Experiences of African American College Students." *Journal of Negro Education* 69(1–2): 60–73.

Stack, Carol. 1974. *All Our Kin: Strategies for Survival in a Black Community.* New York: Basic Books.

Strauss, Anselm L. 1987. *Qualitative Analysis for Social Scientists.* New York: Cambridge University Press.

Sue, Derald Wing. 2010. *Microaggressions in Everyday Life: Race, Gender, and Sexual Orientation.* Hoboken, NJ: Wiley.

Thompson, Maxine S., and Verna M. Keith. 2004. "Copper Brown and Blue Black: Colorism and Self Evaluation." In *Skin Deep: How Race and Complexion Matter in the "Color-Blind" Era*, edited by Cedric Herring, Verna M. Keith, and Hayward Derrick Horton, 45–64. Urbana: University of Illinois Press.

Tuerkheimer, Deborah. 1997. "Street Harassment as Sexual Subordination: The Phenomenology of Gender-Specific Harm." *Wisconsin Women's Law Journal* 12: 167–206.

Venkatesh, Sudhir Alladi. 2006. *Off the Books: The Underground Economy of the Urban Poor.* Cambridge, MA: Harvard University Press.

Washington, Ebonya. 2006. "The Impact of Banking and Fringe Banking Regulation on the Number of Unbanked Americans." *Journal of Human Resources* 41(1): 106–137.

Wesely, Jennifer K. 2006. "Considering the Context of Women's Violence: Gender, Lived Experiences, and Cumulative Victimization." *Feminist Criminology* 1(4): 303–328.

West, Candace, and Sarah Fenstermaker. 1995. "Doing Difference." *Gender and Society* 9(1): 8–37.

———. 2002a. "Accountability and Affirmative Action: The Accomplishment of Gender, Race, and Class in a University of California Board of Regents Meeting." In Doing *Gender, Doing Difference: Inequality, Power and Institutional Change*, edited by Sarah Fenstermaker and Candace West, 141–168. New York: Routledge.

———. 2002b. "Power, Inequality, and the Accomplishment of Gender: An Ethnomethodological View." In *Doing Gender, Doing Difference: Inequality, Power and Institutional Change*, edited by Sarah Fenstermaker and Candace West, 41–54. New York: Routledge.

West, Candace, and Don Zimmerman. 2002. "Doing Gender." In *Doing Gender, Doing Difference: Inequality, Power and Institutional Change,* edited by Sarah Fenstermaker and Candace West, 3–24. New York: Routledge.

Whyte, William Foote. 1993. *Street Corner Society: The Social Structure of an Italian Slum.* 4th ed. Chicago: University of Chicago Press.

Wilkins, Amy C. 2008. *Wannabes, Goths, and Christians: The Boundaries of Sex, Style, and Status.* Chicago: University of Chicago Press.

Williams, Patricia J. *The Alchemy of Race and Rights.* Cambridge, MA: Harvard University Press, 1991.

Wilson, William Julius. 1980. *The Declining Significance of Race: Blacks and Changing American Institutions.* Chicago: University of Chicago Press.

———. 1987. *The Truly Disadvantaged: The Inner City, the Underclass, and Public Policy.* Chicago: University of Chicago Press.

———. 1996. *When Work Disappears: The World of the New Urban Poor.* New York: Vintage.

Index

ABOUT THE AUTHOR

ALEXIS S. MCCURN is an associate professor of sociology at California State University, Dominguez Hills.